First Print Edition [1.0] -1433 h. (2012 c.e.)

Copyright © 1433 H./2012 C.E.
Taalib al-Ilm Educational Resources

http://taalib.com
Learn Islaam, Live Islaam.ˢᴹ

All rights reserved, this publication may be not reproduced, stored in a retrieval system, or transmitted in any form or by any means, electronic, mechanical, photocopying, recording, scanning, or otherwise, except with the prior written permission of the Publisher.

Requests to the Publisher for permission should be addressed to the Permissions Department, Taalib al-Ilm Educational Resources by e-mail: **service@taalib.com**.

Taalib al-Ilm Education Resources products are made available through distributors worldwide. To view a list of current distributors in your region, or information about our distributor/referral program please visit our website. Discounts on bulk quantities of our products are available to community groups, religious institutions, and other not-for-profit entities, inshAllaah. For details and discount information, contact the special sales department by e-mail: **service@taalib.com**.

The publisher requests that any corrections regarding translations or knowledge based issues, be sent to us at: **service@taalib.com.** Readers should note that internet web sites offered as citations and/or sources for further information may have changed or no longer be available between the time this was written and when it is read. We publish a variety of full text and free preview edition electronic ebook formats. Some content that appears in print may not be available in electronic book versions.

ISBN EAN-13:   978-1-938117-42-8   [Soft cover Print Edition]

From the Publisher

GOLDEN WORDS UPON GOLDEN WORDS...FOR EVERY MUSLIM.

"Imaam al-Barbahaaree, may Allaah have mercy upon him said:

May Allaah have mercy upon you! Examine carefully the speech of everyone you hear from in your time particularly. So do not act in haste and do not enter into anything from it until you ask and see: Did any of the Companions of the Prophet, may Allaah's praise and salutations be upon him, speak about it, or did any of the scholars? So if you find a narration from them about it, cling to it, do not go beyond it for anything and do not give precedence to anything over it and thus fall into the Fire.

Explanation by Sheikh Saaleh al-Fauzaan, may Allaah preserve him:

'Do not be hasty in accepting as correct what you may hear from the people especially in these later times. As now there are many who speak about so many various matters, issuing rulings and ascribing to themselves both knowledge and the right to speak. This is especially the case after the emergence and spread of new modern day media technologies. Such that everyone now can speak and bring forth that which is in truth worthless; by this meaning words of no true value - speaking about whatever they wish in the name of knowledge and in the name of the religion of Islaam. It has even reached the point that you find the people of misguidance and the members of the various groups of misguidance and deviance from the religion speaking as well. Such individuals have now become those who speak in the name of the religion of Islaam through means such as the various satellite television channels. Therefore be very cautious!

It is upon you oh Muslim, and upon you oh student of knowledge individually, to verify matters and not rush to embrace everything and anything you may hear. It is upon you to verify the truth of what you hear, asking, 'Who else also makes this same statement or claim?', 'Where did this thought or concept originate or come from?', 'Who is its reference or source authority?'. Asking what are the evidences which support it from within the Book and the Sunnah? And inquiring where has the individual who is putting this forth studied and taken his knowledge from? From who has he studied the knowledge of Islaam?

Each of these matters requires verification through inquiry and investigation, especially in the present age and time. As it is not every speaker who should rightly be considered a source of knowledge, even if he is well spoken and eloquent, and can manipulate words captivating his listeners. Do not be taken in and accept him until you are aware of the degree and scope of what he possesses of knowledge and understanding. As perhaps someone's words may be few, but possess true understanding, and perhaps another will have a great deal of speech yet he is actually ignorant to such a degree that he doesn't actually posses anything of true understanding. Rather he only has the ability to enchant with his speech so that the people are deceived. Yet he puts forth the perception that he is a scholar, that he is someone of true understanding and comprehension, that he is a capable thinker, and so forth. Through such means and ways he is able to deceive and beguile the people, taking them away from the way of truth.

Therefore what is to be given true consideration is not the amount of the speech put forth or that one can extensively discuss a subject. Rather the criterion that is to be given consideration is what that speech contains within it of sound authentic knowledge, what it contains of the established and transmitted principles of Islaam. As perhaps a short or brief statement which is connected to or has a foundation in the established principles can be of greater benefit than a great deal of speech which simply rambles on, and through hearing you don't actually receive very much benefit from.

This is the reality which is present in our time; one sees a tremendous amount of speech which only possesses within it a small amount of actual knowledge. We see the presence of many speakers yet few people of true understanding and comprehension.' "

[The eminent major scholar Sheikh Saaleh al-Fauzaan, may Allaah preserve him- 'A Valued Gift for the Reader Of Comments Upon the Book Sharh as-Sunnah', page 102-103]

My Hijaab, My Path
Pocket Edition
1.
Conditions of Hijaab

Translated & Compiled By
Umm Mujaahid Khadijah Bint Lacina
al-Amreekiyyah as-Salafiyyah

Table of Contents

Pocket Edition Intro -8
About the Compiler & Translator -10
Publisher's Introduction - 12
Compiler's Introduction - 18

Conditions of the Legislated Hijaab according to Sheikh al-Albaani, along with Proofs (may Allaah have mercy upon him) -26

Fifty Authentic Ahaadeeth Concerning the Legislated Hijaab -38

Common Excuses of those who Alter or Abandon the Hijaab, & a Short Reminder -74

This pocket edition is a selection taken from the larger book:

My Hijaab, My Path

SCAN WITH SMARTPHONE

FOR MORE INFORMATION

SCAN WITH SMARTPHONE

FOR MORE INFORMATION

EDITION

A Comprehensive Knowledge Based Compilation on Muslim Women's Role & Dress

Collected and Translated by
Umm Mujaahid Khadijah Bint Lacina
al-Amreekiyyah

|Available: **Now**| pages: **190+** |
price: (Soft cover) **$17.50** |
(Hard cover) **$25** |
eBook **$9.99**

About the Compiler & Translator

The compiler of this work, Umm Mujaahid Khadijah Bint-Lacina, was raised in a small town in the heartland of middle America. She graduated with honors from the University of Wisconsin only a short time after embracing Islaam and starting to live her life as a committed Muslim. She has been blessed with eight Muslim children she is committed to raising, and is regularly involved in various endeavors to benefit herself, fulfill the responsibility to her household, as well as her community and this blessed Ummah. Additionally, she has, in the years before traveling overseas to seek knowledge of this religion, previously run two successful small business enterprises from home - despite her main occupation as a Muslim mother and wife.

By Allaah's mercy she has been studying Islaam and the Arabic language generally since the time she embraced Islaam almost twenty years ago, and both of these subjects intensively for the past nine years from scholars and students of knowledge in the various centers of learning in Yemen and through the books and recorded lectures of the scholars of the Sunnah from throughout the world. Related to her studies in Arabic, she successfully completed two independent study seminars from the Islamic University of Medina while in the United States before having been blessed with the opportunity to study in Yemen. After beginning her language studies in Yemen with the well-known University of Medina Arabic language series through a private tutor, she then built upon this with the study of related classical works of Arabic Grammar when she started studying at Dar Al-Hadeeth in Mab'ar as well as other recommended works with a focus on works related to the fundamental beliefs of Islaam.

She later was blessed to continue her studies of this deen for three years in Dar Al-Hadeeth in Damaaj where she benefited from several excellent teachers. Among them was her daily class with Umm Salamah, may Allaah preserve her, previously the wife of Sheikh Muqbil, with whom in daily study she completed the work Bulugh al-Maram with the exception of two individual chapters due to illness. There she also benefited from the weekly class of the daughter of Sheikh Muqbil, Umm 'Abdullah, and from the lectures of well-known scholars of Ahlis Sunnah throughout Yemen who would come to address the students at the center. She has always striven to benefit from the people of knowledge in every city where her family resided in Yemen, while always making her home the center of her efforts to both study and teach this perfect religion.

May Allaah forgive us, her, and all the Muslims their errors and shortcomings, and guide us to every matter of belief, statement, and action that pleases Him alone.

Publisher's Introduction

All praise is due to Allaah, Lord of the Worlds, peace and salutations be upon the Messenger of Allaah, his household, his Companions, and all those who follow his guidance until the day of Judgment. To proceed:

In today's world few people would deny that the struggle between western ideals and concepts and the religion of Islaam is expanding and intensifying. The so-called 'war against terrorism' is by design a very pliant and indefinable undertaking, which is said to confront any entity, potential or actual, that threatens modern western societies. Yet the claim often put forward, that they fight not against Islaam, but only against 'extremism'- rings incredibly hollow, as many people increasingly realize that the form of Islaam that they deem as 'acceptable' to them, and 'suitable to modern times', on one hand, and the understanding of Islaam encompassed within the beliefs and commands explicitly found in the Qur'aan, on the other, are two incompatible and contradictory visions. Indeed the Qur'aan, which is acknowledged by all Muslims to be one of the enduring, unalterable sources of Islaam, clearly and explicitly informs us of the true primary motivation, as well as the mechanisms and objectives of those who disbelieve in Islaam in their continuing efforts at both the personal and societal level to combat against and suppress that "Qur'anic" version of the religion of Islaam, Indeed, the Lord of the Worlds states very clearly,

❁ *And they will never cease fighting you until they turn you back from your religion -if they can. And whosoever of you turns back from his religion and dies as a disbeliever, then his deeds will be lost in this life and in the Hereafter, and they will be the dwellers of the Fire. They will abide therein forever.* ❁-(Surah al-Baqarah: 217). The noble scholar Imaam as-Sa'dee, may Allaah have mercy upon him, explained part of this verse saying,

"The Most High informs us that the disbelievers will never cease fighting against the believers. And their goal is not taking their wealth or killing them; indeed their primary goal is to force them to abandon and turn away from their religion, in order that they eventually become disbelievers after having already practiced the faith of Islaam, which would lead them to also become people of the Hellfire like those disbelievers. They exert all their efforts and capacity towards achieving that objective. Yet we are informed of what, in actuality, they are and are not capable of, as Allaah states, ❦ **But Allaah will bring His Light to perfection even though the disbelievers hate this.** ❦ *-(Surah As-Saff: 8)*

And this is a general description of every disbeliever. They do not cease opposing and fighting others, until they have actually succeeded in making them abandon and turn away from the religion they once stood upon. And it applies especially to the people of the previous revealed scriptures, from the Jews and Christians. Those who spend significantly upon their worldwide organizations and foundations, sending forth callers to propagate their beliefs, sending forth doctors to work in different lands, building schools- all in an effort to attract and win over the peoples of various nations to their religion, and introduce and plant their foreign religion among these different peoples in their lands. They utilize every matter, and put forth every effort within their capacity, to plant and give rise to doubts among those targeted people which would cause them to have misgivings and uncertainties about the truth of their religion...."

This is indeed the reality in which the person of insight sees us standing in the midst of today. Furthermore there is no issue of engagement related to these numerous battles in the present day ideological warfare against Islaam which carries as much open intensity and passion on both sides as the Muslim woman's hijaab and its predominant place as a symbol of the adherence to or abandonment of Islaam as a way of life.

It has been five years since the democratic government of France banned the individual practice of any Muslim woman resident of that land, from wearing personal clothing that included any recognizable form of hijaab in schools and other indicated areas of public life. Yet many Muslims were genuinely surprised in the face of this explicit assault against their "personal rights" as individual citizens and residents in a western democratic country to practice their religion without infringing upon others in any way or form. These Muslims failed to realize what conforms with what Allaah has stated clearly, that the people who would support such measures simply oppose our very way of life, oppose any concrete expression of a distinct and all-encompassing religious identity, and actually desire that we slowly turn away from any comprehensive form of Islaam which may, even potentially, lead to it being increasingly reflected inwardly and outwardly in the individual and collective lives of Muslim women the world over. This is unfortunately true despite the ever echoing assertions of a commitment to "freedom", "liberty", "self determination", and the "right to individual self expression" which western nations claim to be the guardians of and which they allegedly hope to "enlighten" the Muslim World with. With this ban on hijaab, and the failure of other western countries to vigorously condemn it, many were in fact saying, "*We believe in freedom...but not that kind of freedom*", "*We support the right of self-determination and personal liberty...well...except in regard to Islaam.*"

This documented and evident reality, the war against hijaab, is seen in today's world at various levels, because of that which it invariably represents. It is one of the many fronts which have been opened directly, and more often indirectly, to struggle against any tangible and consistent expression of independent identity by today's Muslims. Their efforts to eradicate and, more significantly, to corrupt and alter hijaab is felt at multiple levels of society, openly and subtly, firstly in their own lands and then additionally as required by their overall objectives, in Muslim countries. Furthermore, their focus upon gradually changing hijaab, and their success in facilitating the adoption of a compromise version of "fashion hijaab", is likewise part of their general attempt to fashion a new "alternate" form of "acceptable" Islaam. Yet in addition to the previously mentioned verse, Allaah has also said to us, *So obey not the deniers. They wish that you should compromise with them, so they too would compromise with you* ﴾-(Surah Qalam: 8-9)

This compilation effectively addresses these defining issues on several levels, including the essential core issue of what is the basis upon which the role and purpose of the Muslim woman is defined- yesterday, today, and tomorrow. Is it the guidance found within the Qur'aan, the eternal, uncreated word of the Creator and Sustainer of the universe and the preserved clarifying example of His Final Messenger (may Allaah's praise and salutations be upon him)? Or is it the newly emergent yet ever changing body of western values based upon a rejection of the true nature of the Qur'aan as revelation? In this work, '*My Hijaab, My Path*' the compiler has done an excellent job of incorporating material that addresses these numerous issues and questions, explains the true guidelines regarding hijaab, and has brought clarity and insight to the principles involved; not merely from opinion, experience, or personal views, but by referring to the works of those people who are the only inheritors and successors of the Last Messenger of Islaam upon earth, the scholars. The scholars referred to are from those known for their depth of knowledge of the sources of Islaam. This book is intended for the Muslim woman who truly wishes to hold fast to the guidance of Islaam, not surrendering it for anyone or anything. Her adherence to Islaam despite the storm of misguidance focused against her, upon sincerity and knowledge, is sufficient for her true success as a believer in Islaam. Due to this, the esteemed scholar Imaam as-Sa'dee concludes his explanation of the first mentioned verse by saying,

"*However, a promise has been given by Allaah the Most High, who is the One who Himself blessed the believers with the religion of Islaam, has chosen for those who believe in Him-this priceless religion, and perfected this religion for them. Indeed, He completed His favor upon them by establishing for them the most valuable of things- their religion. Similarly He abandons and turns away from everyone who desires to extinguish the light of His true religion, and causes their intrigues to become caught in their very throats- while bringing victory to His religion and elevating His word. And certainly these verses correctly reflect the true state of the disbelievers, meaning those who are present today from them,* ❧ *Verily, those who disbelieve spend their wealth to hinder people from the Path of Allaah, and so will they continue to spend it. But in the end it will become an anguish for them, and then they will be overcome. While those who disbelieve will gathered in Hell.* ❧-(Surah Al-Anfal: 36)"

As such, victory in confronting the war against hijaab has already been won by every believing woman who acknowledges the true sources of Islaam, and then learns and practices, upon evidence, each aspect of the guidance of Islaam as found in the Book of Allaah, and the authentic Sunnah of her Prophet ﷺ. Victory has already been given to her by Allaah The Exalted, in her efforts to adhere to the noble examples of the first believers, men and women, and firmly and steadily follow in their footsteps. We hope that the publication of this book acts as a small support and assistance in that for every sincere Muslim woman who truly wants that victory. And the success is from Allaah.

> *Abu Sukhailah Khalil Ibn-Abelahyi*
> *Taalib al-Ilm Educational Resources*

Compilers Introduction (Pocket Edition)

All praise is due to Allaah Alone. We praise Him, seek His help, and ask His forgiveness. We seek refuge in Allaah from the evil of our souls, and the adverse consequences of our deeds. Whomsoever Allaah guides, there is none who can misguide him, and whoever He misguides, there is none who can guide him.

I bear witness that there is nothing worthy of worship except for Allaah; He is alone and has no partners. I bear witness and testify that Muhammad, may Allaah's praise and salutations be upon him and his family, is His perfect worshipper, and messenger.

Oh you who believe! Fear Allaah, as He deserves, and die not except as Muslims. -(Surat al-'Imraan, Ayat 102)

Oh mankind! Fear your Lord, Who created you from a single soul, and from him, He created his wife, and from these two, He created multitudes of men and women. Fear Allaah, from Whom you demand your mutual rights, and do not cut off the ties of kinship. Verily, Allaah is Ever-Watcher over you. -(Surat an-Nisaa', Ayat 1)

Oh you who believe! Fear Allaah, and say righteous speech. He will direct you to do righteous deeds, and He will forgive you your sins. And whoever obeys Allaah and His Messenger has indeed achieved the ultimate success. -(Surat al-Ahzaab, Ayat 70-71)

As to what follows: then the best of speech is the speech of Allaah, and the best guidance is the guidance of Muhammad, may Allaah's praise and salutations be upon him and his family. And the worst of affairs are newly invented matters (in the religion), and every newly invented matter is a misguidance, and every misguidance is in the Hellfire.

To Proceed:

Alhamdulillah, let us look again at the words of the Prophet, may Allaah's praise and salutations be upon him and his family, above:

"The best of speech is the speech of Allaah, and the best guidance is the guidance of Muhammad", may Allaah's praise and salutations be upon him and his family.

These are the sources from which we must take our religion. The Book of Allaah, and the Sunnah of His final Messenger, Muhammad ibn 'Abdullah, may Allaah's praise and salutations be upon him and his family- and we base our understanding of these things on the understanding of the righteous predecessors of the first three generations, alhamdulillah, rather than on our own understandings. The people who may claim this are many, and yet many of them are not actually calling to the true religion of Islaam. Rather, they are calling to Islaam based on their ideas and desires, an Islaam which they twist and mold into the form that best suits their goals, and the goals of the enemies of Islaam, and ultimately, the goals of the accursed *Shaytaan*.
How then, do we know who is calling to the true Islaam?

It is important to understand that, though there is a lot of confusion in the Muslim world, and has been throughout its history, there has always been a group of people that has continued upon the Straight Path of Islaam, as revealed by Allaah to his last Prophet and Messenger, Muhammad ibn 'Abdullaah, praise and salutations be upon him. Distinguished scholars such as Imaam al-Bukhaaree, Imaam Muslim, Imaam Ahmad Ibn Hanbal, Imaam ash-Shaafi'ee, Imaam Maalik, Imaam ash-Shawkaani, Ibn Katheer, and others have carried the banner of Islaam through the ages so that today we can still follow our religion as it was revealed, in all of its perfection, alhamdulillah.
Allaah, the Most High, says in His Noble Book, *This day I have perfected your religion for you, completed My Favor upon*

you, and have chosen for you Islaam as your religion ❩-(Surat al-Maaidah, from Ayat 3)

Allaah gave us our religion in its complete and perfect form- it is not for us to change or recreate it to fit our own ideas and desires, or to conform to the "norm" of the societies around us.

Allaah perfected Islaam for us, and He has always sent people throughout the ages to make sure that the religion is preserved in the form in which it was revealed and originally practiced. This group has many names, including *Ahl-as-Sunnah wa al-Jamaa'ah*, and *as-Salafiyyeen*, but the important thing is that they adhere to the Qur'aan as well as the Sunnah of Prophet Muhammad, praise and salutations be upon him, according to the understanding of the first three generations of Islaam. These were the people who were nurtured at the hand of Allaah's Messenger, praise and salutations be upon him, and his Companions, and so on down through the generations. And, as we must understand the *deen* of al-Islaam with the proofs, I will mention some of them here.

First, from the book of Allaah; *al-Haafidh* ibn Katheer mentions in his *tafseer* of the Qur'aan the explanation of the verse regarding the one who leaves the way of the first believers, which is found in Surat an-Nisaa':

❨ *And whoever contradicts and opposes the Messenger after the right path has been shown clearly to him, and follows other than the believers' way, We shall keep him in the path he has chosen, and burn him in Hell. What an evil destination!*❩ -(Surat an-Nisaa', Ayat 115)

❨ *And whoever contradicts and opposes the Messenger after the right path has been shown clearly to him.*❩ *This refers to whoever intentionally takes a path other than the path of the Law revealed to the Messenger, after the truth has been made clear, apparent and plain to him.*

Allaah's statement, ❲...and follows other than the believers' way...❳ refers to a type of conduct that is closely related to contradicting the Messenger. This contradiction could be in the form of contradicting a text (from the Qur'aan or Sunnah) or contradicting what the ummah (nation) of Muhammad has agreed on. The ummah of Muhammad is immune from error when they all agree on something, a miracle that serves to increase their honor, due to the greatness of their Prophet. There are many authentic ahaadeeth on this subject.

Allaah warned against the evil of contradicting the Prophet and his ummah, when He said, ❲We shall keep him in the path he has chosen, and burn him in Hell- what an evil destination!❳ meaning, when one goes on this wicked path, We will punish him by making the evil path appear good in his heart, and will beautify it for him so that he is tempted further."

The Messenger of Allaah, praise and salutations be upon him and his family, made clear the importance of adhering to his guidance and that of the rightly guided predecessors in the following authentic hadeeth, on the authority of al-Irbaad ibn Saaryah who said, *{Allaah's Messenger, may Allaah's praise and salutations be upon him, gave us an admonition which caused our eyes to shed tears and the hearts to fear, so we said, "O Messenger of Allaah, may Allaah's praise and salutations be upon him, this is as if it were a farewell sermon, so with what do you counsel us?"*
So he, may Allaah's praise and His salutations be upon him, said, I have left you upon clear guidance, its night is like its day, no one deviates from it except one who is destroyed, and whoever lives for some time from amongst you will see great differing. So stick to what you know from my Sunnah and the Sunnah of the rightly guided caliphs. Cling to that with your molar teeth, and stick to obedience even if it is to an Abyssinian slave since the believer is like the submissive camel;

wherever he is led, he follows.}

(An authentic hadeeth found in *"Sunan Abu Daawood"* 4607, *"Sunan Ibn Majah"* 43 and 44, *"Sunan at-Tirmidhi"* 2676, *"al-Musnad Ahmad"* vol. 4/126 and other collections. The wording is that of at-Tirmidhi)

And in another authentic hadeeth:

{My ummah will split into seventy three sects, all of them in the Fire except one and it is al-Jamaa'ah.} It was said, "Who are they, O Messenger of Allaah?" He, praise and salutations be upon him, replied, {That which I and my Companions are upon today.}

(Authentic hadeeth reported by at-Tirmidhi (no.2643), al-Laalikaa'ee in *"as-Sunnah"* (no.147) and others)

We can see how the Companions, may Allaah be pleased with all of them, realized this in their lives, by looking at the following *athaar* from their time, may Allaah be pleased with all of them.

'Amr ibn Salmah said: We used to sit by the door of 'Abdullah ibn Mas'ood before the morning prayer, so that when he came out we would walk with him to the masjid. One day Abu Moosaa al-Ash'aree came to us and said, "Has Abu 'Abdur-Rahman come out yet?" We replied, "No." So he sat down with us until he came out. When he came out, we all stood along with him, so Abu Moosaa said to him, "O Abu 'Abdur-Rahman! I have just seen something in the mosque which I deemed to be evil, but all praise is for Allaah, I did not see anything except good." He inquired, "Then what is it?" (Abu Moosaa) replied, "If you live you will see it. I saw in the masjid people sitting in circles awaiting the prayer. In each circle they had pebbles in their hands and a man would say 'Repeat Allaahu Akbar a hundred times.' So they would repeat

it a hundred times. Then he would say, 'Say laa ilaaha illallaah a hundred times.' So they would say it a hundred times. Then he would say, 'Say subhaanallaah a hundred times.' So they would say it a hundred times." (Ibn Mas'ood) asked, "What did you say to them?" (Abu Moosaa) said, "I did not say anything to them. Instead I waited to hear your view or what you declared." (Ibn Mas'ood) replied, "Would that you had ordered them to count up the evil deeds they acquired and assured them that their good deeds would not be lost!"

Then we went along with him (Ibn Mas'ood) until he came to one of these circles and stood and said, "What is this which I see you doing?" They replied, "O Abu 'Abdur-Rahman! These are pebbles upon which we are counting takbeer, tahleel and tasbeeh." He said, "Count up your evil deeds. I assure you that none of your good deeds will be lost. Woe to you, O ummah of Muhammad, praise and salutations be upon him! How quickly you go to destruction! These are the Companions of your Prophet and they are widespread. There are his clothes which have not yet decayed and his bowl which is unbroken. By Him in Whose Hand is my soul! Either you are upon a religion better guided than the Religion of Muhammad, praise and salutations be upon him, or you are opening the door of misguidance." They said, "O Abu 'Abdur-Rahman! By Allaah, we only intended good." He said, "How many there are who intend good but do not achieve it. Indeed Allaah's Messenger said to us, "A people will recite the Qur'aan but it will not pass beyond their throats." By Allaah! I do not know, perhaps most of them are from you." Then he left them.

Umar ibn Salmah (the sub-narrator) said: We saw most of those people fighting against us on the day of Nahrawaan, along with the Khawaarij.

(Ad-Daarimi in his *"Sunan"* (1/79) Authenticated by Sheikh Saleem al-Hilaalee)

One of the loudest calls today, from the disbelievers as well many misguided individuals within Islaam, is that call to change the *hijaab*, or the Muslim women's dress, or to discard it all together. People with no firm grounding in religious knowledge write books and articles concerning women in the Qur'aan, or the rights of the Muslim women, and they base that which they present upon their own intellect, ideas, and desires, as well as upon that which was said by ignorant, misguided, or evil people other than them, who have been falsely held up as scholars amongst the people. The vast majority of these writers and callers make a point of addressing the issue of the *hijaab* directly. Often they claim it is not from Islaam, or that the form it takes today in many Muslim countries such as Saudi Arabia and Yemen is extreme and unnecessary. This is despite the clear evidences to the contrary, evidences that anyone with a sound intellect can read and understand.

I ask that Allaah correct my mistakes, preserve my intention, and accept this work from me, and I pray that the Muslim *ummah* in general, and my Muslim sisters specifically, benefit from it.

Any good in this work is from Allaah, alone, who has no partners, and any evil is from myself and the accursed *Shaytaan*.

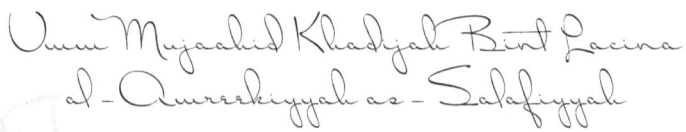

Umm Mujaahid Khadijah Bint Lacina al-Amreekiyyah as-Salafiyyah

Conditions of the Legislated Hijaab according to Sheikh al-Albaani, along with Proofs (may Allaah have mercy upon him)

As compiled and explained in the book, "Waajibaat al-ar'at al-Muslimah" by Umm 'Amr bint Ibraaheem Badawiyyah, with a preface by Sheikh Muqbil ibn Haadee al-Wadi'ee, may Allaah have mercy upon him

From the mercy of Islaam to the woman is that it does not leave off anything which will rectify her, except that it has legislated it, and guided to it, and commanded her to follow it. Additionally, it does not leave anything and any matter which harms her, except that it warns her against it, and prohibits her from it.

From that which is clear from that which Allaah, Glorified and Exalted is He, has legislated, and through it her standing is elevated, and her position raised, is that when she has attained the age of maturity and reason, she must cover her body, and leave off revealing her beauty when she leaves her house- and to guide the Muslim women to veil themselves.

Likewise, she should stay in her house, as it is from those things which conceal her (*al-hijaab*).

Allaah, the Most High, says, ❴ *And stay in your houses, and do not display yourselves like that of the times of ignorance* ❵- (Surat al-Ahzaab, From Ayat 33)

And the Most High says, ❴ *And tell the believing women to lower their gaze (from looking at forbidden things), and protect their private parts (from illegal sexual acts) and not to show off their adornment except that which is apparent (like both eyes for necessity to see the way, or outer palms of hands or one eye or outer garment) and to draw their veils all over juyubihinna (i.e. their bodies, faces, necks and bosoms) and not to reveal their adornment except to their husbands, or their fathers, or their husband's fathers, or their sons, or their husband's sons, or their brothers or their brother's sons, or their sister's sons, or their women, or the (female) slaves whom their right hands possess, or old male servants who lack sexual desire, or small children who have no sense of feminine sex. And let them not stamp their feet so as to reveal what they hide of their adornment.* ❵- (Surat an-Noor, From Ayat 31)

And the Most High says, ⦃ *O Prophet! Tell your wives and your daughters and the women of the believers to draw their cloaks (veils) all over their bodies. That will be better that they should be known (as free respectable women) so as not to be harassed.*⦄-(Surat al-Ahzaab, From Ayat 59)

The Islamically Legislated *Hijaab* has Conditions

It is obligatory for the Muslim woman that she be distinguished by that which the verses which are mentioned by the Most Wise, and which the Sunnah of the Messenger, may Allaah's praise and salutations be upon him, are proofs for. And they are as follows: (The footnote in the text here reads, "The best of the speech upon this matter is that of the Imaam of our time, Sheikh Naasir ad-Deen al-Albaani, may Allaah, the Most High, have mercy upon him, in his book, "*Hijaab al-Mar'at al-Muslimah*", along with that we differ with him in his opinion that it is permissible to uncover the face and hands)

1. That the Legislated Hijaab Covers the Entire Body

As in the statement of *al-Haqq*, Exalted is He, Most High, ﴿ *O Prophet! Tell your wives and your daughters and the women of the believers to draw their cloaks (veils) all over their bodies. That will be better that they should be known (as free respectable women) so as not to be harassed. And Allaah is Ever Oft-Forgiving, Most Merciful.* ﴾ - (Surat al-Ahzaab, Ayat 59)

In this verse is a clear indication upon nothing being visible of beauty and adornment except in the state of *al-ihraam* (for *hajj* or *umrah)*

(Translator's Note: The author's footnote mentions here the hadeeth of 'Aishah mentioned in "Fifty Ahaadeeth…" which has been included in this compilation. See Number 12 for full information and the text of the hadeeth)

Also, that which al-Bukhaaree has narrated in his "*Saheeh*" from the hadeeth of Ibn 'Umar, may Allaah be pleased with both him and his father, in which he said, *{Allaah's Messenger, may Allaah's praise and salutations be upon him, said, (concerning the woman who is making hajj or 'umrah), "The woman should not use a veil to cover her face and should not wear gloves."}*.

And that he, may Allaah's praise and salutations be upon him, said, *{The woman is 'awrah; for if she goes out the Shaytaan elevates her (in the eyes of others).}* (From the hadeeth of 'Abdullah Ibn Mas'ood, Number 22 in "Fifty Ahaadeeth…")

2. That the Hijaab be Thick, not Transparent or Thin

From his, may Allaah's praise and salutations be upon him, saying, in the hadeeth of Abi Hurairah, may Allaah be pleased with him, in which he said, *{ There are two types of the people of the fire who I did not see: A people having whips like oxtails with them, with which they beat the people, and women who would be dressed yet appear naked, who would be inclined to evil and incite others towards it. Their heads are like the humps of camels, inclined to one side. They will not enter Paradise, nor smell its fragrance, though its fragrance be detectable from such and such a far distance.}* (See Number 29 of "Fifty Ahaadeeth...")

Imaam an-Nawawi, may Allaah, the Most High, have mercy upon him, said, *"This hadeeth is from the miracles of the Prophethood, as these two types of people have already come to be, and they are found (in society today); and in it (the hadeeth) these two types of people are censured. It is said that its meaning is that they are dressed out of the beneficence of Allaah, and naked, or bereft, of gratitude for His blessing. And it is said that it means that she covers part of her body, while uncovering some of it, displaying it through its condition and manner of being worn. And it is said that it means that she is wearing dresses which are thin, and describe the color of her skin. And as for "maa'ilaat" (inclining), she is walking in swaggering manner, inclining or swaying her shoulders. And it is said, she is combing her hair in an inclining fashion and it is the style of the prostitute, thus this fashion inclines other than them to it. And the meaning of their heads being like the humps of camels is that they make it large and grand, wrapping it into a turban or head cloth or that which resembles them."* (End of quote from Imaam an-Nawawi's explanation of "*Saheeh Muslim*")

And all of these meanings which have been mentioned have occurred in this time in which we live. And to Allaah alone can we complain of the people of this time.

3. That the Hijaab not be Attractive or Beautiful in and of Itself

This is taken from the saying of Allaah, the Most High, ⟨*...and not to show off their adornment...*⟩- (Surat an-Noor, from Ayat 31)

The statement here is general, and includes under it that which is attractive in and of itself, or which is beautified with something, drawing attention by it, and drawing the gaze to it.

Imaam adh-Dhahabi, may Allaah have mercy upon him, said, *"From the actions which the woman will be cursed for is displaying the adornments, gold, and pearls from under the veil, as well as perfuming herself with musk and amber and that which is like that. Also, she wears the colorings (make up) and the deceitful things and that which resembles that from that which is scandalous."* (End of quote from *"al-Kabaa'ir"*, page 102)

The Esteemed Scholar ash-Shawkaani, may Allaah have mercy upon him, said, in explanation of the saying of the Most High, ⟨*...and not to show off their adornment...*⟩, that it means that which they beautify themselves with from jewels and decorations and other than them, and that included in the prohibition of showing off their adornment is the prohibition of displaying the beauty of their bodies to an even greater degree. (Taken from *"Fath al-Qadeer"*, vol. 4, page 13)

4. The Hijaab must be Loose Fitting and Wide, not Tight and Narrow so that Anything from her Body is Defined

The case may be that the clothing may be loose fitting, while at the same time it is sheer or partially transparent- and this is not permitted because the purpose of the garment is to eliminate temptation, and this is not done except with the loose fitting, wide garment which does not expose anything from her body, and likewise does not describe the size of her body, as it is apparent to the men.

It has been related from Usaama ibn Zaid, that he said, *{The Messenger of Allaah gave me a thick Qabaati garment, and it was from the things that Dihya Al-Kalbi gave him, so I gave it to my wife to wear. The Messenger of Allaah, may Allaah's praise and salutations be upon him, said to me, "What is wrong with you, that you do not wear the garment?" I said, "Oh Messenger of Allaah, I gave it to my wife to wear. He said, "Order her that she wear beneath it an undergarment as I am afraid that it will describe her figure."}* (Reported by Ahmad and at-Tabaraanee in *"al-Kabeer"* and in it is 'Abdullah ibn Muhammad 'Aqeel, and his hadeeth is closer to being weak)

The Scholar, ash-Shawkaanee, may Allaah have mercy upon him, said, *"This hadeeth is a proof that it is obligatory upon the woman to cover her body with a garment that does not define her figure. And this is a condition of her covering the 'awrah. And he commanded that she wear a garment under it because the "qabaatee"* (قباطي) *is a flimsy garment which does not cover the person from the vision of the one who is looking at it; rather, it defines her.* (From *"Nayl al-Awtaar"*, 2/117)

The women of this time must fear Allaah from their wearing of the narrow garments which could perhaps cut into their bodies from their tightness. They must remember the saying of the Messenger of Allaah, may Allaah's praise and salutations be upon him, *{All of modesty is goodness.}* (al-Bukhaaree, Muslim, Abu Daawood, and Ahmad)

5. The Legislated Hijaab must not be Scented or Perfumed

Because of what is in that of affecting the men, as seen in his, may Allaah's praise and salutations be upon him, saying in a hadeeth of Abi Moosaa al-Ash'aree, may Allaah be pleased with him, when he said, *{The woman who is perfumed and passes by the sitting, then she is such and such...}* Meaning, she is an adulteress. (Abu Daawood, an-Nasaa'i, at-Tirmidhi, who declares it to be *hasan saheeh*, and Ibn Khuzaimah, and al-Haakim, and it is authentic, and all praise is due to Allaah)

His saying in the hadeeth of Zainab ath-Thaqafiyyah, may Allaah be pleased with her, 'Allaah's Messenger, may Allaah's praise and salutations be upon him, said, *{If one of you (women) attends the masjid, then do not wear perfume.}* Zainab ath-Thaqafiyyah: She is Zainab bint Mu'aawiyyah, or the daughter of 'Abdullah ibn Mu'aawiyyah, and it is said, she is the daughter of Abu Mu'aawiyyah ath-Thaqafiyyah, the wife of 'Abdullah ibn Mas'ood, and a Companion whose hadeeth are found in the Six Books of Hadeeth. (Biographical information taken from "*Taqreeb at-Tahdheeb*" No. 8598) (Muslim, an-Nasaa'i)

As this (the *masjid*) is the house of Allaah, the Most High, so what about you all who go out scented to the street, or the market or other than them?!?

There is no doubt or uncertainty that their ruling is stronger in forbiddance, and Allaah knows best.

6. The Woman's Clothing must not Resemble that of the Man

Verily the woman who wears the clothing which is worn by the men, does something which is contradictory to that nature which Allaah has made her natural disposition, and she does that which is contrary to modesty, and there is no doubt that this is forbidden.

Ibn 'Abaas, may Allaah be pleased with him, said, *{The Messenger of Allaah, may Allaah's praise and salutations be upon him, cursed the men who resemble the women, and the women who resemble the men.}* (al-Bukhaaree, Abu Daawood, at-Tirmidhi, who declared it *hasan saheeh*, and Ibn Maajah, Ahmad, ad-Daarimee, and an-Nasaa'i in "*'Ashrat an-Nisaa*")

7. That the Women's Clothing not Resemble the Clothing of the Disbelieving Women

This is what the wise legislation forbids us from. It is that which the Messenger of Allaah, may Allaah's praise and salutations be upon him, was speaking of, when he said, *{He who resembles a people is one of them.}* (Abu Daawood, Ahmad, Sa'eed ibn Mansoor, and al-Qadaa'ee. Ibn Taymiyyah, may Allaah have mercy upon him, said, "Its chain of narrations is good." in "*al-Iqtidaa*", page 72)

Sheikh al-Islaam, Ibn Taymiyyah, may Allaah have mercy upon him, said, *"This hadeeth, the least of its conditions is that it requires that resembling them is forbidden, and its apparent meaning is that it demands that the one who resembles them has disbelieved, as is found in His saying, the Most High, ﴿ And if any amongst you takes them as Auliyaa' (friends, protectors, helpers) then surely, he is one of them.﴾* -(Surat al-Maa'idah, From Ayat 51) "He (Ibn Taymiyyah, may Allaah have mercy upon him), then said, *"And through this, more than one of the scholars has made it a requirement that things from the clothing of other than the Muslims are disliked."*

Muhammad ibn Harb said, *"I asked Ahmad* (meaning, Ahmad ibn Hanbal, may Allaah have mercy upon him) *concerning Sindee shoes, and going out in them. He disliked it for the man and the woman. And he said, "If it is for the bathroom or the wudhoo, then there is no problem with it, and I dislike the sound it makes (like a cricket)"* And he said, *"It is from the clothing of the foreigners."*

Sa'eed ibn 'Aamir (it is found in *"at-Tabaqaat"* of Ibn Sa'ad, that he is Abu Muhammad al-Basree, the abstemious one, the memorizer, who was born in 120 *Hijree* and died in 208 *Hijree*) was asked concerning it, and he said, *"The Sunnah of our Messenger, may Allaah's praise and salutations be upon him, is more beloved to us than the Sunnah of Baakahun."* And Baakahun was the ruler of India at that time. (From *"al-Iqtidaa"* page 84)

The prohibition of resembling them (the disbelievers) is an unrestricted prohibition. 'Umar ibn al-Khattab, may Allaah be pleased with him, wrote to the leader of the Muslim army in *Adhrabeejaan* on the lack of resembling them, as he said, *"Beware of the clothing and shoes of the people of shirk and the silk garment..."* to the end of the hadeeth. (Narrated by Muslim)

So we are a people whom Allaah has strengthened with His correct and sound *deen* (religion, way of life- Islaam), and from its distinguishing characteristics is its clothing, which Allaah is pleased with for us. And the one who wishes to resemble us, then welcome, and welcome, as we are on the truth and the merit, as long as we follow the Book and the Sunnah; and those besides us are on falsehood and are mistaken, due to their distance from the Book and the Sunnah and their taking passing fancies and desires. Because of that, we do not resemble other than us.

﴿ *Has not the time come for the hearts of those who believe (in the Oneness of Allaah – The worship of Allaah alone without associates) to be affected by Allaah's Reminder (this Qur'aan), and that which has been revealed of the truth, lest they become as those who received the Scripture before (i.e. Jews and Christians), and the term was prolonged for them and so their hearts were hardened? And many of them were the rebellious, the disobedient to Allaah.* ﴾
-(Surah Hadeed, Ayat 16)

8. That the Clothing not be Clothing of Fame or Notoriety

This is whether that which is intended is showing off its high price, or to demonstrate one's asceticism in order to show off for others; as both of these are prohibited. As it is related from the Messenger of Allaah, may Allaah's praise and salutations be upon him, in the hadeeth of Ibn 'Umar, may Allaah be pleased with both him and his father, that he said, *{The one who wears a garment of fame in this world, then Allaah will clothe him in a garment of humility on the Day of Resurrection then he will be set aflame in it in the Fire.}* (Abu Daawood, Ibn Maajah, Ahmad, and Sheikh al-Albaani has declared it to be *hasan*, in *"al-Hijaab"* and *"Saheeh Sunan Ibn Maajah"*

The Esteemed Scholar ash-Shawkaani, may Allaah have mercy upon him, said, *"The hadeeth is a proof for the prohibition of wearing the clothing of fame. This hadeeth is not specific to costly garments. Rather, that may also occur in the one who wears a wretched, inferior garment which differs from the people's clothing in order to be seen by the people so they are surprised or amazed by his clothing and they believe him. Ibn Raslaan said this.*

If it is worn with the intention of gaining notice or fame amongst the people, then there is no difference between the exalted garments or the humble ones, and that which is approved by the people or which differs from them, because the prohibition revolves around the fame or glory, and the significant thing is the intention, even if it does not match the reality. (*"Nayl al-Awtaar"*)

Ibn Taymiyyah, may Allaah have mercy upon him, said, *"Seeking fame or notoriety by the clothing is something hated. And it is something that is higher than the normal clothing or lower than the normal clothing. As the Salaf used to dislike both of these things, both raising and lowering."* (*"Majmoo' al-Fataawa"*)

Fifty Authentic Ahaadeeth Concerning the Legislated Hijaab

Originally Collected by Umm Usaama bint 'Ali al-'Abaasi, Dar al-Hadeeth, Damaaj; With Additions by the Translator

HADEETH

Chapter 1:
How the Verse of the Hijaab was Revealed

1. *{ Related Anas Ibn Maalik, may Allaah be pleased with him, that he was a boy of ten years when the Messenger of Allaah, may Allaah's praise and salutations be upon him and his family, came to Medina. "My mother placed me in his service. I served him for ten years, and he died when I was twenty years old. So I am the most knowledgeable amongst the people concerning the matter of the hijaab. It first descended when the Messenger of Allaah, may Allaah's praise and salutations be upon him and his family, built a house for Zainab Bint Jahsh. He celebrated the wedding feast there, and he called the people and they came and partook of the food. They then left, and a few stayed with the Prophet, may Allaah's praise and salutations be upon him and his family, and prolonged their visit. So he (the Prophet, may Allaah's praise and salutations be upon him and his family) stood up and left, and I left as well, in order that they would leave. He walked, and I walked with him, until he reached the door of 'Aishah's chamber. When he thought the guests had left, he returned, and I returned with him, until he went in to where Zainab was, and they were still sitting there. So he left, and I left with him, walking to the door of 'Aishah's chamber. When he thought they had left, he returned, and I returned with him, and they had indeed left. Then the Prophet, may Allaah's praise and salutations be upon him and his family, drew between me and him a covering, and the verses about hijaab were revealed. }*

> (Collected by al-Bukhaaree in "*al-Adab al- Mufrad*", No. 1083, and in his "*as-Saheeh*", vol. 8, No. 4793, and Muslim in his "*Saheeh*", vol. 2, No. 1428)

2. *{'Aishah, may Allaah be pleased with her, narrated that the wives of Allaah's Messenger, may Allaah's praise and salutations be upon him and his family, used to go out at night if they needed to relieve themselves, to open fields outside of Medina. 'Umar Ibn al-Khattab said to the Messenger of Allaah, may Allaah's praise and salutations be upon him and his family, "You should cover your wives." The Messenger of Allaah, may Allaah's praise and salutations be upon him and his family, did not do that. So Sawdah Bint Zamah, a wife of the Prophet, may Allaah's praise and salutations be upon him and his family, went out at night when it was dark. She was a tall woman. 'Umar called out to her, "Oh Sawdah! We recognize you!" hoping that the verses of the hijaab would descend. 'Aishah said, "Then Allaah, Exalted and Glorified, revealed the hijaab.}*

> (Collected by al-Bukhaaree, vol. 8, No. 4795, and Muslim, vol. 4, No. 18-2170, and it is his wording.)

3. Also on 'Aishah, may Allaah be pleased with her, that she said, *{ I was eating with the Prophet, may Allaah's praise and salutations be upon him and his family, some 'hees' from a wooden bowl. He saw 'Umar, may Allaah be pleased with him, and invited him to eat with us, and he ate. Our fingers hit each other, and he ('Umar) said, "I felt your fingers!" and so he made a disapproving moaning sound, and said, "If I had my way it would be that you were not seen at all!" And then ayat of the hijaab was revealed }"*

> (Collected by at-Tabarani in "*al-Mu'jam as-Sagheer*" vol. 1, page 83. Our Sheikh, Abu 'Abdur-Rahman, Muqbil Ibn Haadee al-Wadi'ee, may Allaah have mercy upon him, mentioned it in "*as-Saheeh al-Musnad min Asbaab an-Nazool*")

HADEETH

Chapter 2:
The Command of the Hijaab

Allaah, the Blessed, the Most High, says, ❮And to draw their veils all over juyubihinna (i.e. their bodies, faces, necks, and bosoms)...❯ -(Surat an-Noor, from Ayat 31)

And He, Exalted be His praise, says, ❮Oh Prophet! Tell your wives and your daughters and the women of the believers to draw their cloaks (veils) all over their bodies (i.e. screen themselves completely except the eyes or one eye to see the way). That will be better, that they should be known (as free, respectable women) so not to be harassed. And Allaah is Oft-Forgiving, Most Merciful❯ -(Surat al-Ahzaab, Ayat 59)

> 4. 'Aishah, may Allaah be pleased with her, narrated: *{May Allaah have mercy on the first al-Muhaajiraat (the early women emigrants to al-Madinah). When Allaah revealed ❮... and to draw their veils all over their juyubihinna...❯ they tore their maroot (general clothing; a dress, or wrap) and placed these as khimaars covering themselves.}*
>
> (Collected by al-Bukhaaree, vol. 8, No. 4758)

And 'Aishah, may Allaah be pleased with her, used to say, *{When this ayat ❮...and to draw their veils over their juyubihinna...❯ was revealed, the women cut their waist-sheets from their seams and used the cut cloths as khimaars to cover themselves}*

5. *{Umm Salamah, may Allaah be pleased with her, narrated: ❴When the verse, "…draw their cloaks over their bodies…❵ was revealed, the women of al-Ansaar (the native women of al-Madinah) went out as if there were black crows upon their heads from their outer garments.}*

> (Collected by Abu Daawood, vol. 4, No. 4101. Sheikh al-Albaani, may Allaah have mercy upon him, graded it as *saheeh* (authentic).)

Chapter 3:
The Obligation of al-Hijaab Applies to Covering in Front of the Good and the Bad People

6. *{ Anas, may Allaah be pleased with him, narrated that 'Umar, may Allaah be pleased with him, said, "I agreed with Allaah in three things." Or, he said, "My Lord agreed with me in three things. I said, 'Oh Allaah's Messenger! Would that you took the place of Ibraaheem as a place of prayer!' I also said, 'Oh Allaah's Messenger! Both good and bad people visit you! Would that you commanded the Mothers of the Believers to veil themselves!' So Allaah revealed the verses pertaining to al-hijaab. It had come to my attention that the Prophet, may Allaah's praise and salutations be upon him and his family, had admonished some of his wives. So I went to them and said, 'You should stop this, or perhaps Allaah will give His Messenger, may Allaah's praise and salutations be upon him and his family, better wives than you!' Until I came to one of his wives, and she said, 'Oh 'Umar! Does not Allaah's Messenger, may Allaah's praise and salutations be upon him and his family, have what he needs to admonish his wives, that you also have to admonish them?' And Allaah revealed, ❴ It may be that if he divorced you all his Lord will give him instead of you Muslim women better than you…❵ -(Surat at-Tahreem, from Ayat 5 to the end.)}*

> (Collected by al-Bukhaaree, vol. 8, No. 4483)

Chapter 4: The Obligation of Investigating the Person whom the Woman Covers From

7. 'Aishah, may Allaah be pleased with her, narrated, *{The Messenger of Allaah, may Allaah's praise and salutations be upon him and his family, entered upon me while a man was with me. He said, 'Oh 'Aishah, who is this?' I said, 'My brother from nursing.' He said, 'Oh 'Aishah! Be certain of who your brothers are by this means, as the nursing relationship is only established if it occurs during the period when the child nurses out of hunger!'}*

> (Collected by al-Bukhaaree, vol. 5, No. 2647, and Muslim, vol. 2, No. 1455)

8. 'Aishah, may Allaah be pleased with her, also said, *{Aflah asked permission to visit me, but I said I did not allow him to enter. He said, 'Do you cover yourself in front of me, even though I am your uncle?' I said, 'How is that?' He replied, 'You were nursed from my brother's wife, with the milk of my brother.' I asked the Messenger of Allaah, may Allaah's praise and salutations be upon him and his family, about that, and he said, 'Aflah is correct. Allow him to visit you.'}*

> (Collected by al-Bukhaaree, vol. 5, No. 2644, and it his wording, as well as by Muslim, vol. 2, No. 1445)

HADEETH

Chapter 5:
The Obligation of Covering in Front of One who there is Doubt as to his Status as a Mahram

9. 'Aishah, may Allaah be pleased with her, narrated that, *{Utbah ibn Abu Waqqas authorized his brother, Sa'd ibn Abu Waqqas, to take the son of Zamah's slave girl into his custody, informing him that the boy was his (Utbah's) son. When the Messenger of Allaah, may Allaah's praise and salutations be upon him and his family, entered Makkah at the time of the conquest, Sa'd took Zamah's son and went with him to the Messenger of Allaah, may Allaah's praise and salutations be upon him and his family. He also took 'Abd, the son of Zamah, with him. Sa'd said, "Oh Messenger of Allaah! This is the son of my brother; he confided to me that he is his son." 'Abd ibn Zamah said, "Oh Messenger of Allaah! This is my brother, son of the slave girl of Zamah, and he was born on his bed." So the Messenger of Allaah, may Allaah's praise and salutations be upon him and his family, looked at the son of the slave girl of Zamah and saw that he resembled him (Utbah) much. Allaah's Messenger, may Allaah's praise and salutations be upon him and his family, said, {He is for you, 'Abd ibn Zamah} by reason that he was born on the bed of his father. The Messenger of Allaah, may Allaah's praise and salutations be upon him and his family, said,' 'Cover yourself from him, oh Sawdah bint Zamah' from what he saw of his resemblance to Utbah, and Sawdah was a wife of the Prophet, may Allaah's praise and salutations be upon him and his family.}*

(Collected by al-Bukhaaree, vol. 5, No. 2533)

Chapter 6:
The Obligation of Covering from the Child, and from the Effeminate Men who are able to Distinguish and Describe the Woman

Allaah, the Most High, says ❴*...or old male servants who lack desire, or small children who have no sense of the feminine sex...*❵ –(Surah an-Noor, from Ayat 13)

10. On 'Aishah, may Allaah be pleased with her, who said, *{An effeminate man used to enter the homes of the wives of the Prophet, may Allaah's praise and salutations be upon him and his family, and they did not object, as they considered him to be without sexual desire. One day Allaah's Messenger, may Allaah's praise and salutations be upon him and his family, entered, and the effeminate man was with some of the women of the Prophet's, may Allaah's praise and salutations be upon him and his family, household. He was describing a woman, and he said, 'When she approaches, there are four curves on her front, and if she turns her back, eight curves appear on her back.' So the Prophet, may Allaah's praise and salutations be upon him and his family, said, 'I see that he is aware of sexual matters, so do not let him visit you.' 'Aishah said, 'So we covered ourselves from him.'}*

(Collected by Muslim, vol. 4, No. 2181)

11. Umm Salamah, may Allaah be pleased with her, narrated that *{The Prophet, may Allaah's praise and salutations be upon him and his family, was with her, and in the house was an effeminate man. He (the man) said to 'Abdullah, the brother of Umm Salamah, 'Oh 'Abdullah! If Ta'if should be conquered tomorrow I recommend to you the daughter of Ghaylaan, for she is so shapely that she has four curves in the front and eight at the back.' So the Prophet, may Allaah's praise and salutations be upon him and his family, said, 'Do not allow these (effeminate men) to enter upon you.'}*

(Collected by al-Bukhaaree, vol. 10, No. 5887, and Muslim, vol. 4, No.2180)

Chapter 7:
The Obligation of Covering the Entire Face from the Non-Mahram Man, and to Drape the Khimaar (headscarf) from above her Head to the Termination of her Neck, when she is in Ihraam

12. It is narrated on 'Aishah, may Allaah be pleased with her, that she said, *{Riders would pass by us and we were in ihraam (for hajj or 'umrah) with the Messenger of Allaah, may Allaah's praise and salutations be upon him and his family. When they drew alongside of one of us, she would let down her outer garments from her head, over her face. When he had passed by, then we would uncover our faces.}*

(Collected by Abu Daawood, vol. 2, No. 1833 "Chapter: A Woman in *Ihraam* Covers her Face". This hadeeth by this specific chain of narration is weak, but it has a support in the narration in the following hadeeth of Asmaa.)

13. Asmaa bint Abi Bakr, may Allaah be pleased with her, said, *{We covered our faces from the men, and combed our hair before that in ihraam.}*

> (Collected by al-Haakim in "*Mustadrak*" vol. 1, No. 1680. He said, "This hadeeth is *saheeh* on the conditions of the two sheikhs (i.e. al-Bukhaaree and Muslim) and they did not collect it." Adh-Dhahabee concurred with this.)

14. It is narrated on 'Aishah, may Allaah be pleased with her, that she said, *{ Oh Messenger of Allaah! Do the people return with the two rewards and I return with only one?" So he commanded 'Abdur-Rahman ibn Abi Bakr to go with her to at-Taneem. She said, "He placed me behind him on his camel. I lifted my head scarf from my neck, and he struck my foot as if he were striking the camel. I said to him, 'Do you see anyone?' She said, "So I entered into the state of ihraam for 'umrah, until we reached the Messenger of Allaah, may Allaah's praise and salutations be upon him and his family, and he was at Hasbah.}*

> (Collected by Muslim, vol. 2, No. 1211)

Chapter 8:
The Characteristics of the Hijaab: That it is Thick and Loose, not Transparently Thin, and Free of Anything that Beautifies the Woman

15. Narrated Umm 'Alqamah: *{Hafsah bint 'AbdurRahman entered upon 'Aishah, the Mother of the Believers, and Hafsah was wearing a thin khimaar." 'Aishah removed it from her and covered her with a thick khimaar.}*

    (Collected by Ibn Sa'd in "*At-Tabaqat al-Kubra*" vol. 8, page 71, from the chain of narration of Umm 'Alqamah. Her name was Marjaanah, and she was the *mawlah* of 'Aishah, and she is truthful and *hasan* narrator in hadeeth.]

16. 'Umar ibn al-Khattab, may Allaah be pleased with him, gave garments to the people of Qubaatee, and then said, "Do not use them for your women's shirts." So a man said, "I dress my women in such as this, but such clothes begin within the house and end there. So I do not see it as too transparent." 'Umar replied, "Even if it is not transparent, it still describes her."

    (Collected by al-Bayhaaqee in "*as-Sunan al-Kubra*" vol. 2, page 235, and its chain of transmission is *hasan (mawqoof)*.)

17. Hisham ibn 'Urwah related that al-Mundhir ibn az-Zubayr arrived from Iraaq and sent to Asmaa bint Abi Bakr some garments from fabric that was elaborately woven and strong, but delicate and thin. After she finished looking it over she felt it with her hand and said, "Ugh! Return his garments to him." This was hard for him to accept, so he came and said to her, "Oh our mother, the clothing is not transparent." She replied, "If it is not transparent, it still describes (that which is under it)." So he purchased for her other garments that were still finely woven and strong, but not thin, which he presented to her, upon which she said, "Clothes such as this are those suitable for me."

> (Taken from Ibn Sa'd in "*At-Tabaqat al-Kubra*" vol. 8, page 252, from the narration of Isma'eel ibn 'Abdullaah ibn Abi Uwais on his father, and both of them are *da'eef* (weak) narrators. However, it is corroborated and supported by the narration mentioned before it (*mawqoof*).)

Chapter 9:
The Characteristics of the Jilbaab: That it is of a Length which Covers the Feet, because they are Considered 'Awrah

18. 'Abdullaah ibn 'Umar, may Allaah be pleased with him, narrated that { *The Prophet, may Allaah's praise and salutations be upon him and his family, said, 'He who drags his garment out of vanity, Allaah does not look at him on the Day of Judgment.' Umm Salamah, may Allaah be pleased with her, said, "And what should the women do with the end of their garments?" He said, 'Lower them a hand span.' She said, "If their feet are still uncovered?" He said, 'Then lower them an arm span, and no further.'* }

> (At-Tirmidhi collected it in vol. 3, No. 1737, from the chain of narration of Nafi' on ibn 'Umar. There is a difference of opinion concerning Nafi', but it is corroborated by the hadeeth of ibn 'Umar that follows.)

19. 'Abdullaah ibn 'Umar narrated that { *The Messenger of Allaah, may Allaah's praise and salutations be upon him and his family, permitted the mothers of the believers, may Allaah be pleased with all of them, to extend the end of their garments a hand span. Then they asked him to increase this amount and he extended it for them an arm span.* }

> (This hadeeth due to supporting narrations. Collected by Abu Daawood, vol. 4, No. 4119, from the narration of Zaid al-'Amee on the authority of Abi as-Sadeeq an-Naajee from ibn 'Umar. And one of the narrators is Zaid al-'Amee, he is ibn al-Hawaaree, Abu al-Hawaaree who is considered weak. But the hadeeth is raised to the level of *hasan* by the hadeeth that precedes it.)

Chapter 10:
On Covering the Hands, because they are 'Awrah (something to be concealed from those men who are not mahram for the woman (i.e. a man that the woman is not forbidden to marry)

20. Umaarah ibn Khazaymah said, "Once we were sitting with 'Amr ibn al-'Aas during *hajj* or *'umrah*, when we were close to a woman who was wearing her jewelry and rings, and she spread out her hand from the *hawdah* (litter or sedan chair). He said, *{ Once we were with the Messenger of Allaah, may Allaah's praise and salutations be upon him and his family, in this mountain pass when suddenly he said, 'Look! Do you see something?' We said, we saw a number of crows and among them was a crow with white feet, a red bill and legs. So the Messenger of Allaah, prayer and salutations be upon him and his family, said, 'Among the women who enter paradise will be those who are like this crow among those crows.'}*

> (Collected by Imaam Ahmad (vol. 4, pages 197 and 205). Sheikh al-Albaani, may Allaah have mercy upon him, mentioned it in "*as-Silsilaat as-Saheeh*" (vol. 4, No. 1850) and he said, This chain is *saheeh* (authentic).)

21. 'Abdullah ibn 'Umar, may Allaah be pleased with him, said, *{ The Prophet, Allaah's praise and salutations be upon him, said concerning the woman who is making hajj or 'umrah, 'The woman should not use a veil to cover her face and should not wear gloves.'}*

Sheikh al-Islaam ibn Taymiyyah, may Allaah have mercy upon him, said, as found in *"Majmoo' al-Fataawa"* (vol. 5, pages 271-272): *"And this is from that which indicates that the veil and the gloves were common for the women who were not in a state of ihram and that it is required that they cover their faces and hands."*

Chapter 11:
In which the Whole of the Woman is 'Awrah

22. 'Abdullah ibn Mas'ood, may Allaah be pleased with him, said, The Messenger of Allaah, Allaah's praise and salutations be upon him and his family, said, *{The woman is 'awrah; for if she goes out the Shaytaan makes her desirable in the eyes of others.}*

> (Collected by at-Tirmidhi in vol. 2, No. 1176. And our Sheikh, Abu 'Abdur-Rahman, al-Wadi'ee, may Allaah have mercy upon him, mentioned it in *"as-Saheeh al-Musnad"*, vol. 2, No. 862, and he said, "This hadeeth is *saheeh* according to the conditions of Imaam Muslim.")

Chapter 12:
Chapter on the Prohibition of the Woman Removing her Garments in other than her own House

23. It is narrated that 'Aishah, may Allaah be pleased with her, said that women from Syria came to her, and she said, "Perhaps you are from the province in which its women enter the public bathhouses?" They said, yes. She said, "Verily, I heard the Messenger of Allaah, Allaah's praise and salutations be upon him and his family, say, *{Any woman who removes her garment in other than her own house, what is between her and between Allaah, Most Exalted, Most High, will be closed off."}*

> (Collected by 'Abdurrazaaq in his "*Musnaf*", vol. 1, page 293, and it is in *"as-Saheeh al-Musnad"* of our Sheikh Abi 'Abdur-Rahman al-Wadi'ee, may Allaah have mercy upon him, vol. 2, No. 1649. He said, "It is a *saheeh* (authentic) hadeeth.")

Chapter 13: The Modesty of the Virgin

24. Narrated on Abi Sa'eed al-Khudree, may Allaah be pleased with him, that he said, *{The modesty of the Messenger of Allaah, Allaah's praise and salutations be upon him and his family, was greater than that of a virgin in her private rooms.}*

    (Collected by al-Bukhaaree, vol. 16, No. 3562, and Muslim, vol. 4. No. 2320)

25. And on Abi Mas'ood, 'Uqbah ibn Amaar, may Allaah be pleased with him, said, "The Prophet, Allaah's praise and salutations be upon him and his family, said, *{Verily, from what the people acquired from the previous prophetic statements is the saying: If you have no shame, then act as you wish.}*

    (Collected by al-Bukhaaree, vol. 6, Numbers 3483 and 3434)

Chapter 14:
Chapter on the Permissibility of Borrowing the Outer Garment

26. It is narrated on Hafsah bint Seereen, that she said, *{On 'Eid we used to prevent our girls from going out for the 'Eid prayer. A lady came and stayed in the palace of Bani Khalaf and I went to her. She said, "The husband of my sister took part in the twelve holy battles along with the Prophet, may Allaah's praise and salutations be upon him and his family, and my sister was with her husband in six of them. My sister said that they used to nurse the sick and treat the wounded. Once she asked, "Oh Allaah's Messenger! If a woman has no outer garment (jilbaab) is there any harm if she does not come out (on the day of 'Eid)?" The Prophet, may Allaah's praise and salutations be upon him and his family, said, 'Her companion should lend her from her own outer garments, and the women should participate in the good deeds and the religious gatherings of the believers.' Hafsah added, "When Umm 'Atiyah came, I went to her and asked her, "Did you hear anything about such and such?" Umm 'Atiyah replied, "Yes, let my father be sacrificed for him (and she never mentioned the name of the Prophet may Allaah's praise and salutations be upon him and his family, except that she would say, "Let my father be sacrificed for him). He, may Allaah's praise and salutations be upon him and his family, said, referring to the categories of women, 'Mature virgin girls staying often screened (or he said, 'Mature girls and virgins staying often screened'- Ayoob (a sub narrator) was not sure which was correct) and menstruating women should come out. But the menstruating women should keep away from the musalla (the actual place of prayer). And all the women should participate in the good deeds and religious gatherings of the believers.' Hafsah said, "On that day I also said to Umm 'Atiyah, "Also those who are menstruating?" Umm 'Atiyah replied, "Yes. Do they not present themselves at 'Arafat and elsewhere?!}*

(Collected by al-Bukhaaree, vol. 2, No. 980, and Muslim, vol. 2, No. 890)

HADEETH

Chapter 15:
On the Prohibition of Going Out Uncovered

Allaah, the Most High, says, ⟨ *And stay in your houses, and do not display yourselves like that of the time of ignorance* ⟩ -(Surat al-Ahzaab, from Ayat 33)

And He, the Most High, says, ⟨ *And as for the women past childbearing years who do not expect to marry, it is no sin on them if they discard their (outer) clothing in such a way so as not to show their adornment. But to refrain (i.e. to not discard their outer clothing) is better for them. And Allaah is All-Hearer, All-Knower.* ⟩ -(Surat an-Noor, Ayat 60)

27. Fadaalah ibn 'Ubayd narrated that the Messenger of Allaah, may Allaah's praise and salutations be upon him and his family, said, *{Three are not to be asked about: A man who separates from the jama'ah (the group of Muslims on the established way of truth) disobeying his Imaam and dying in disobedience, a female or male slave who runs away and then dies in this state, and a woman whose husband is away and he supplies her with all necessary provisions, yet she goes out uncovered after he leaves. And three are not even to be asked about: A man who competes with Allaah, Glorified and Exalted, disputing concerning His garment, as Allaah's garment is His Grandeur and His izaar (waist wrap) is His Glory, a man who doubts the command of Allaah, and the one who has lost hope in the Mercy of Allaah.}*

> (Collected by Imaam Ahmad, vol. 6, page 19, and al-Bukhaaree in "*al-Adab al-Mufrad*", Number 603. It is also in "*as-Saheeh al-Musnad*" of our Sheikh, Abi 'Abdur-Rahman al-Wadi'ee, may Allaah have mercy upon him, vol. 2, No. 1054. He said, this hadeeth is authentic (*saheeh*).)

28. 'Amr ibn Shu'ayb narrated on his father, who narrated on his ('Amr's) grandfather (and he is 'Abdullaah ibn 'Amr ibn al-'Aas) that he said: "Umaymah bint Raqeeqah went to the Messenger of Allaah, may Allaah's praise and salutations be upon him and his family, to give allegiance to Islaam. He said, *{I will take your pledge to not associate anything with Allaah, and to not steal, and to not commit fornication, and to not kill your children, and that you not utter slander (meaning by causing illegally conceived children to be attributed to your husband) and to not wail over the dead, and to not go out uncovered like the going out of the pre-Islamic time of ignorance.}*" (see Surat Mumtahinah, Ayat 12)}

(Collected by al-Imaam Ahmad, vol. 2, page 192, with a *hasan* chain of narrators)

Chapter 16:
What has come Concerning the Women who will be Dressed but Appear Naked, who Incline to Evil and Incite Others to Evil

29. Abu Hurairah, may Allaah be pleased with him, reported that Allaah's Messenger, may Allaah's praise and salutations be upon him and his family, said, *{There are two types of the people of the fire who I did not see: A people having whips like oxtails with them, with which they beat the people, and women who would be dressed yet appear naked, who would be inclined to evil and incite others towards it. Their heads are like the humps of camels, inclined to one side. They will not enter Paradise, nor smell its fragrance, though its fragrance be detectable from such and such a far distance.}*

(Collected by Muslim, vol. 3, Number 2128)

HADEETH

A Great Point of Benefit

al-Imaam al-Qurtubee, may Allaah have mercy upon him, said, in his "*Tafseer*", vol. 12, page 309:

""At-tabaruj': being exposed and visible to the eyes.

And from it: constructed high towers, and the constellations in the heavens. There is no barrier besides it, covering it. Then it is said, from "at-tabaruj" is the woman wearing two transparent garments which show her clearly. It is narrated in the "Saheeh" (of Imaam Muslim, may Allaah have mercy upon him) that Abu Hurairah, may Allaah be pleased with him, said that the Messenger of Allaah, may Allaah's praise and salutations be upon him and his family, said, "There are two types of the people of the fire who I did not see: A people having whips like oxtails with them, with which they beat the people, and women who would be dressed yet appear naked, who would be inclined to evil and incite others towards it. Their heads are like the humps of camels, inclined to one side. They will not enter Paradise, nor smell its fragrance, though its fragrance be detectable from such and such a far distance." Ibn al-Arabee said, "They are dressed because they are wearing clothes; and they are described as being naked because the nature of the dress is thin and describes them and makes their beauty apparent, and that is prohibited."

I say: This is one of the explanations of the scholars concerning this meaning. The second: That they are wearing clothes, but they are not wearing the clothing of piety, about which Allaah, Most High, says, ﴾...and the raiment of righteousness, that is better...﴿ (Surat al-A'raaf, from Ayat 26)

If the person never wears the raiment of piety
 He changes to being naked, even if he is clothed
The best clothing for man is obedience to his Lord
 And there is no good for the one who disobeys Allaah

In "Saheeh Muslim", on the authority of Abi Sa'eed al-Khudree, may Allaah be pleased with him, that the Messenger of Allaah, may Allaah's praise and salutations be upon him and his family, said, {While I was asleep I saw people being presented to me (in a dream). They wore shirts, some of which reached the breast and some that were other than that. 'Umar ibn al-Khattab passed by, and his shirt trailed down him.} They said, "How do you interpret that, Oh Messenger of Allaah?" He said, {Faith (religion).} ("Saheeh Muslim", No. 2390)

So the Messenger of Allaah, may Allaah's praise and salutations be upon him and his family, interpreted the shirt as being faith, derived from the saying of the Most High, ❮...and the raiment of righteousness, that is better...❯

And the Arab is known for modesty and decency in dressing. As the poet said, "The clothing of the tribe of 'Awf is pure and clean."

And he, may Allaah's praise and salutations be upon him and his family, said to 'Uthman, {Verily Allaah is going to dress you in a shirt. Indeed they want you to remove it- then don't remove it.}"

> (Tirmidhi, No. 3705, Ibn Majah on 'Aishah, No. 112, "*Musnad*" al-Imaam Ahmad) The shirt here indicates the *khaleefah* (ruler of the Muslims), and it is a well known metaphor.)

I say: This interpretation is the best of these two interpretations; it reflects their state (the women) in this age, especially the young women. Indeed, they beautify themselves and go out of their houses adorned; so, they are wearing clothes, but are lacking true piety- that which is the outward or apparent expression of it, as well as its inward reality. Such that they display their physical beauty, without any concern about who looks at them. Rather, that is their goal, which is born witness by that which they present outwardly; for if they had any degree of fear of Allaah or piety when they approached that, then they would not act in this manner. From that which will help you understand this, and which strengthens this interpretation, is that which is mentioned describing them in the rest of the hadeeth, in his, may Allaah's praise and salutations be upon him and his family, saying, {Their heads are like the heads of camels}, citing the example of the camel- the body's bones, the bones of the hump. Their heads resemble it by way of them raising the braids of their hair to the middle of their heads, and this is a well-known sight, and when seen is clearly recognized.

The Messenger of Allaah, may Allaah's praise and salutations be upon him and his family, said, {There will not remain after me a trial more harmful to the men, than the women.}" (Collected by al-Bukhaaree)"

(End of quote from "*Al-Jaameea Lil Ahkaam al-Qur'aan*")

Chapter 17:
From the Hijaab is that the Woman Walks with a Quiet, Soft Step and does not Wear Shoes that make a Noise like High Heels, and without Swaying and Swinging

Allaah says, ﴾*...And let them not stamp their feet so as to reveal what they hide of their adornment. And all of you beg Allaah to forgive you all, Oh believers, that you may be successful*﴿ -(Surat an-Noor, from Ayat 31)

And The Most High says, ﴾*And walk not on the earth with conceit and arrogance. Verily, you can neither rend nor penetrate the earth, nor can you attain a stature like the mountains in height.*﴿ -(Surat al-Isra', Ayat 37)

And it is related on Luqman, upon him be Allaah's salutations, ﴾*And turn not your face away from men with pride, nor walk in insolence through the earth. Verily, Allaah likes not any arrogant master . And be moderate (or show no insolence) in your walking, and lower your voice. Verily the harshest of all voices is the braying of the donkey.*﴿ -(Surat Luqman, Ayat 18-19)

And Allaah the Most High, Most Exalted, says, ﴾ *And the (faithful) slaves of the Most Gracious (Allaah) are those who walk on the earth in humility and sedateness, and when the foolish address them (with bad words) they reply back with mild words of gentleness.*﴿ -(Surat al-Furqan, Ayat 63)

30. Abu Sa'eed al-Khudree narrated that the Prophet, may Allaah's praise and salutations be upon him and his family, said, *{'There was a woman from Banee Israa'eel who was short. She was walking with two tall women. She then took elevated sandals of wood (to wear) and made part of a ring of pure gold to be able to hold something within it, which she then filled with musk, and musk is the best of all fragrances. She later walked again between the two women, and the people did not recognize her at that time. She gestured like this with her ringed hand.' Then Shu'bah (a sub narrator) shook his hand (to show how the woman gestured.}*.

(Collected by Muslim, vol. 4, Number 2252)

Chapter 18:
The Woman Remaining in her House and not going out Except for her Needs

Allaah, the Most High, the Most Exalted, says, ⦃*And stay in your houses, and do not display yourselves like that of the times of ignorance, and perform as-Salaat and give zakaat and obey Allaah and His Messenger…*⦄ (from Surat al-Ahzaab, Ayat 33)

31. Abu Hurairah, may Allaah be pleased with him, narrated that the Messenger of Allaah, may Allaah's praise and salutations be upon him and his family, when he made his *hajj* with his wives, said, *{Verily, what this is, is a necessity; afterwards the period of their emerging and being out will be restricted or limited.}*

(Collected by al-Imaam Ahmad, vol. 2, page 446, with a *hasan* chain of narration)

32. 'Aishah, may Allaah be pleased with her, said, *{ Sawdah bint Zamah went out at night for a need, and 'Umar saw her and recognized her. He said to her, "By Allaah, Oh Sawdah, you cannot hide yourself from us." She returned to the Prophet, may Allaah's praise and salutations be upon him and his family, and mentioned that to him while he was eating supper in my house. He had at that time a bone covered with meat. The Divine revelation came down upon him, and when it was lifted, the Prophet may Allaah's praise and salutations be upon him and his family, was saying, ⌐ Allaah has allowed you to go out for your needs.⌐}*

(Collected by al-Bukhaaree, vol. 9, No. 5237)

Chapter 19:
The Prayer of the Woman in her House is Better than her Prayer Elsewhere, and if she goes to the Prayer in the Masjid she should do so Properly Covered. However, her House is Better for Her

33. 'Abdullah bin Mas'ood narrated that the Prophet, may Allaah's praise and salutations be upon him and his family, said, *{The woman's prayer in her house is more excellent than her prayer in her courtyard, and her prayer in her private chamber of her house is more excellent than her prayer in her house.}*

(Collected by Abu Daawood, vol. 1, No. 570, and it is in "*as-Saheeh al-Musnad*" of our Sheikh, Abu 'Abdur-Rahman al-Wadi'ee, may Allaah have mercy upon him, vol.2, No. 847, and he said, "This hadeeth is *saheeh* on the conditions of Muslim.")

34. Abu Hurairah, may Allaah be pleased with him, said that the Messenger of Allaah, may Allaah's praise and salutations be upon him and his family, said, *{Do not prevent the female servants of Allaah from the masaajid of Allaah, but they may only go to them if they have not perfumed themselves.}*

> (Collected by Abu Daawood, vol. 1, No. 565, and it is in "*as-Saheeh al-Musnad*" vol. 2, No. 1288)

35. Ibn 'Umar, may Allaah be pleased with him, said that Allaah's Messenger, may Allaah's praise and salutations be upon him and his family, said, *{Do not prevent the female servants of Allaah from the masjid, but their houses are better for them.}*

> (Collected by Abu Daawood, vol. 1, No. 567, and Sheikh al-Albaani, may Allaah have mercy upon him, declared it *saheeh* (authentic) in "*Saheeh Abu Daawood*")

36. 'Aishah, may Allaah be pleased with her, said, "If Allaah's Messenger, may Allaah's praise and salutations be upon him and his family, had known what the women are doing now (seen what new things the women have introduced into their way of life), he would certainly have forbidden them (from going out to the *masaajid*), just as the women of Bani Israa'eel were forbidden."

(Translator's Note: The first part of this hadeeth, which the sister did not quote in her collection, is as follows: 'Aishah, may Allaah be pleased with her, said that, *{The Prophet would offer the Fajr prayer (in congregation) and then witness that the believing women, wrapped up with their shawls, had prayed with him. They would then return to their homes, and no one would recognize them due to the darkness.}* To the end of the hadeeth. Sheikh al-Utheimeen, may Allaah have mercy upon him, pointed out in his "A Short Treatise on *Hijaab*", *"The observance of the hijaab and the covering of the face were of the customary practices of the female companions. They were the best and most honorable of all generations, in the sight of Allaah. They possessed the highest and most superior characteristics and manners, as well as the most complete eemaan (faith) and the purest of actions. They are the role models of whom Allaah is pleased with and with whosoever follows them in righteousness..."*) (End translator's note)

(Collected by al-Bukhaaree, vol. 2, No. 869, and Muslim, vol.1, No. 445)

Imaam an-Nawawi, may Allaah have mercy upon him, said in his explanation of the hadeeth of 'Aishah, "*He would have forbidden them...' means from improper beautification, and perfume, and wearing attractive garments. And Allaah knows best.*"

Chapter 20: Concerning the Prohibition of the Intermixing of the Women and Non-Mahram Men, and that there is not for the Woman except the Sides of the Road

37. Abu Usaid al-Ansaaree, may Allaah be pleased with him, said that he heard the Messenger of Allaah, may Allaah's praise and salutations be upon him and his family, saying when he was leaving the *masjid* and the men and women were mingling in the road: *{The Messenger of Allaah, may Allaah's praise and salutations be upon him and his family, said to the women, 'Draw away, for it is not for you to have the right of the path (meaning, it is not for you to travel in the middle of it). It is upon you to keep to the sides of the road.' The women then stayed so close to the walls that their garments rubbed against them."}*

> (Collected by Abu Daawood, vol. 4, No. 5272, and its chain is made *hasan* by the following supporting hadeeth.)

38. Abu Hurairah, may Allaah be pleased with him, said that the Messenger of Allaah, may Allaah's praise and salutations be upon him and his family, said, *{The middle of the path is not for the women.}*

> (Narrated by Ibn Hibban, vol. 12, No. 5601, and its chain is made *hasan* by other supporting narrations.)

HADEETH

Chapter 21: The Prohibition of the Woman Looking at the Men who are not Mahram for Her

Allaah, the Most High, says, ❮ *And tell the believing women to lower their gaze (from looking at forbidden things) and protect their private parts (from illegal sexual acts)…* ❯ -(Surat an-Noor, from Ayat 31)

And Allaah, the Most High, says, ❮ *…Verily the hearing, and the sight, and the heart, of each of those will be questioned (by Allaah)* ❯ -(Surat al-Israa', from Ayat 36)

And the Most High says, ❮ *Allaah knows the fraud of the eyes, and all that the breasts conceal.* ❯ -(Surat al-Ghaafir, Ayat 19)

39. Abu Hurairah, may Allaah be pleased with him, narrated that the Prophet, may Allaah's praise and salutations be upon him and his family, said, *{Allaah has written for the sons of Aadam his inevitable share of adultery that will not be avoided. The adultery of the eye is the looking (at that which it is unlawful to look at), and the adultery of the ears is listening (to that which it is unlawful to hear), and the adultery of the tongue is the speech (that which it is unlawful to say), and the adultery of the hand is oppression, and the adultery of the leg is to walk (to that which is impermissible), and the heart desires and yearns (for that which is impermissible) and the private parts turn that into reality or refrain from it.}*

(Collected by al-Bukhaaree, vol. 11, No.6612, and Muslim, vol.3, No. 2657, and the wording is his)

40. Jareer ibn 'Abdullaah said, {*I asked the Messenger of Allaah, may Allaah's praise and salutations be upon him and his family, about the unexpected glance (meaning at a woman). He commanded me to turn my eyes away.*}

(Collected by Muslim, vol. 3, No. 2159)

Chapter 22:
The Prohibition of the Woman Shaking Hands with a Man who is a Stranger to Her

41. Umaymah bint Raqeeqah said, {*I made the oath of allegiance to Allaah's Messenger, may Allaah's praise and salutations be upon him and his family, with the women. So he, may Allaah's praise and salutations be upon him and his family, instructed us in that which you are able to do and are able to endure. I said, "Allaah and His Messenger are more merciful than us on our own selves." I said, "Oh Messenger of Allaah, we give the oath of allegiance to you." He said, 'Verily, I do not shake the hands of the women. Truly, that which I have said to one woman is like my saying it to one hundred women.'*}

On Umaymah bint Raqeeqah at-Taymiyyah, that she said, {*I came to Allaah's Messenger, may Allaah's praise and salutations be upon him and his family, with women from the Muslims in order to give him the oath of allegiance. So we said, "Oh Messenger of Allaah, we have come to give the oath of allegiance to you, that verily we do not associate with Allaah anything, and we do not steal, and we do not commit fornication, and we do not kill our children, we will not utter slander, intentionally forging falsehood (i.e. by causing illegal conceived children to be attributed to their husbands) and we will not disobey you in ma'roof (the worship of Allaah alone and all that Allaah ordains.)"*}

(Translator's note: see Surat al-Mumtahanah, Ayat 12) *Allaah's Messenger, may Allaah's praise and salutations be upon him and his family, said, 'In that which you are able to do, and are able to endure.' She said, "We said, 'Allaah and His Messenger are more merciful with us, than we are to ourselves. We give our oath of allegiance to you, Oh Messenger of Allaah.'" He said, 'Go, for you have made the pledge. Verily my saying to one hundred women is like my saying to one woman.' She said, "And Allaah's Messenger, may Allaah's praise and salutations be upon him and his family, did not shake the hands of the women.}*

(Collected by Imaam Ahmad in his "*Musnad*", vol. 6, No. 357, and it is in "*as-Saheeh al-Musnad*" by our Sheikh, Abu 'Abdur-Rahman al-Wadi'ee, may Allaah have mercy upon him, vol.2, No. 1557)

42. 'Aishah, may Allaah be pleased with her, a wife of the Prophet, may Allaah's praise and salutations be upon him and his family, said, *{Allaah's Messenger, may Allaah's praise and salutations be upon him and his family, used to interrogate the believing women who emigrated to him in accordance with this verse: ﴿ Oh Prophet! When believing women come to you to five the bai'a (oath of allegiance) to you...﴾ up to His saying, ﴿ ...Oft Forgiving, Most Merciful ﴾ Urwah (the sub narrator) said, 'Aishah said, "And if any of the believing women accepted the condition (mentioned in the verse), Allaah's Messenger, may Allaah's praise and salutations be upon him and his family, would say to her, 'I accept your oath.' He would say that, and, by Allaah, his hand never touched the hand of the woman during the pledge. He did not accept their pledge, except through saying, 'I have accepted your oath in that.'}*

(Collected by al-Bukhaaree, vol. 8, No. 4891)

Chapter 23:
The Prohibition of the Woman being Secluded with a Non-Mahram Man, and the In-Laws are Death

Allaah the Most High says, ❴*...and when you ask (his wives) for anything that you want, ask them from behind a screen; that is purer for your hearts and their hearts.*❵ (Surat al-Ahzaab, from Ayat 53)

43. 'Uqbah ibn 'Amir, may Allaah be pleased with him, narrated that the Messenger of Allaah, may Allaah's praise and salutations be upon him and his family, said, *{'Beware of entering upon the women.' A man from the Ansaar said, "Oh Allaah's Messenger! What about al-Hamoo (the in-laws)?" He, may Allaah's praise and salutations be upon him and his family, said, 'al-Hamoo are death.'}*

    (Collected by al-Bukhaaree, vol. 9, No. 5232, and Muslim, vol. 4, No. 2172; and he added, "*al-Hamoo*" is the brother of the husband, and those similar blood relations from the husband's family, such as the uncle's son and like him.)

44. Ibn 'Abbas, may Allaah be pleased with him, narrated that the Prophet, may Allaah's praise and salutations be upon him and his family, said, *{'No man should be in seclusion with a woman except in the presence of one who is mahram for her.' A man stood up and said, "Oh Messenger of Allaah! My wife has gone out to perform the hajj and I am enrolled in the army for such and such campaign." The Prophet, may Allaah's praise and salutations be upon him and his family, said, 'Return, and perform the hajj with your wife.'}*

    (Collected by al-Bukhaaree, vol. 9, No. 233, and Muslim, vol. 2, No. 1341)

Chapter 24:
The Prohibition of the Woman Touching the Man who is not Mahram for her- like the Female Doctors, Nurses, and Like Them

45. Ma'qul ibn Yasaar said, the Messenger of Allaah, may Allaah's praise and salutations be upon him and his family, said, *{That a man is pierced in the head with a steel needle is better for him than that he touches a woman who is not permissible for him.}*

    (Collected by ar-Roowaanee in his "*Musnad*", vol. 2, No. 1283, and Sheikh al-Albaani, may Allaah have mercy upon him, mentioned it in "*as-Silsilaat as-Saheeh*", vol. 1, No. 226, and he said, "This chain of narration is *hasan*.")

Chapter 25:
A Woman should not Look at or Touch the Body of another Woman to Describe her to her Husband

46. 'Abdullaah ibn Mas'ood, may Allaah be pleased with him, said, the Prophet, may Allaah's praise and salutations be upon him and his family, said, *{A woman should not intimately look at or touch the body of another woman, and then describe her to her husband in such a way as if he were looking at her.}*

    (Collected by al-Bukhaaree, vol. 9, No. 240)

All praise is due to Allaah Alone, Who completes by His Blessing good deeds, and His praise and salutations be upon the best of His Messengers Muhammad, and on his family, and companions, and the best praise be upon them."

Some Additional Ahaadeeth Concerning the Hijaab and the Prohibition of Free Mixing Between the Sexes, Added by the Translator

47. Abu Hameed, may Allaah be pleased with him, reported that the Prophet, may Allaah's praise and salutations be upon him and his family, said, *{ When one of you (believers) intends to marry a woman, there is no sin on him if he looks at her, as long as his looking at her is only for the purpose of the intention of marriage. And this is even if she is unaware of it. }*

(Collected by Imaam Ahmad in his "*Musnad*", and Sheikh al-Albaani, may Allaah have mercy upon him, declared its chain of narration authentic in "*as-Saheehah*", No. 97)

48. Anas ibn Maalik, may Allaah be pleased with him, narrated that the Prophet, may Allaah's praise and salutations be upon him and his family, said, *{ If it comes about that one of you (female companions) is with a slave who has entered into an agreement to purchase his freedom and can pay the full price for it, then observe the hijaab in front of him.}*

(Collected by Imaam Ahmad in his "*Musnad*", Abu Daawood, Ibn Majah, and at-Tirmidhi, who authenticated it.)

49. Nafi' reported from Ibn 'Umar that the Messenger of Allaah may Allaah's praise and salutations be upon him and his family, said, *{Let us leave this door (of the masjid) for the women.}* Nafi' said, "So Ibn 'Umar did not enter through this door until he died.

> (Collected by Abu Daawood, and Sheikh al-Albaani authenticated it.)

50. Umm Salamah, may Allaah be pleased with her, said that, *{In the time of Allaah's Messenger, may Allaah's praise and salutations be upon him and his family, when the women would make tasleem to finish the obligatory prayer (in congregation), they would get up to leave, and Allaah's Messenger, may Allaah's praise and salutations be upon him and his family, and the men who had prayed with him would remain in their places for as long as Allaah willed. When he would get up, then the men would get up.}*

> (Collected by al-Bukhaaree, vol. 1, No. 825)

Common Excuses of those who Alter or Abandon the Hijaab, & A Short Reminder

Physical Excuses:

Hijaab will make my hair fall out
Hijaab will make me look fat
I have asthma, or allergies, or thyroid problems, or am claustrophobic
Hijaab impedes my movements
I am still young, and *hijaab* is the dress of old women
It is too hot to wear *hijaab*

Work Excuses:

I will not be able to get a job if I wear *hijaab*
Hijaab makes my work difficult for me
I will be fired if I wear *hijaab*

Personal Excuses:

Hijaab will enslave me, and make me lose my freedom
Hijaab will cause me to be disrespected
Hijaab will cause me to be discriminated against or attacked
I give a lot of *da'wah*, and if I wear *hijaab* it will scare people away
I do not like *hijaab* because some of the women who wear it have bad manners
Hijaab will make me lose my individuality
I will not be able to get married if I cover my beauty
I will wear *hijaab* after my engagement
I will wear *hijaab* after I am married, so that I can wear what I like at my wedding
If I wear *hijaab* my husband will be attracted to other women

I am ashamed to wear *hijaab* in front of my friends
Hijaab is more expensive than other clothing, so I cannot afford it
My parents or husband forbid me from wearing *hijaab*, so how can I disobey them?

Ideological Excuses:

I do a lot of good deeds, and my heart is filled with faith, so what do my clothes have to do with it?
I am not sure about *hijaab*- is it obligatory or is it only a Sunnah?
I believe in and work for women's rights, and going without *hijaab* is what distinguishes us
I want to be like the Westerners, or else I will be called "old fashioned"
Going without *hijaab* does not draw attention or affect anyone; rather, it has become common
We have to be modern, and stay with the times, and *hijaab* is something from the past
There is no basis for *hijaab* in Islaam; it is a cultural thing
There is no reason for extremism, as our religion is one of ease

A Reminder to my Sisters

So look through these excuses, my sisters in Islaam, and see which of them you or your sisters may have used at one time or another, and ask yourself the question, "Is this really a valid excuse?" And how do you know if it is, indeed, a valid one? You must ask the people of knowledge specifically about your case, as they have the knowledge and the wisdom to answer you so that there is no doubt. Indeed, many of these doubts and misconceptions have been addressed in this compilation, alhamdulillah, and their paucity and lack of substance made clear by the people of knowledge in our time and in the past.

Think carefully, and take an accounting of yourself, as we are commanded with obedience to Allaah and His Messenger, may Allaah's praise and salutations be upon him.

Allaah says in His Book,
❴ *Surely, the religion (i.e. the worship and the obedience) is for Allaah only...* ❵-(Surat az-Zamr, from Ayat 3)

And He, the Most High, says, ❴ *And turn in repentance and in obedience with true Faith (the worship of Allaah alone without associates) to your Lord and submit to Him (in Islaam) before the torment comes upon you, (and) then you will not be helped.* ❵-(Surat az-Zumar, from Ayat 54)

And His saying, ❴ *And who can be better in religion than one who submits his face (himself) to Allaah (i.e. follows Allaah's religion of worshiping Him alone without associates); and he is a Muhsin (a good-doer)* ❵-(Surat an-Nisaa', from Ayat 125)

And He, the Most High, says, ❴ *And whosoever submits his face (himself) to Allaah, while he is a Muhsin (good-doer, i.e. performs good deeds totally for Allaah's sake without any show-off or to gain praise or fame and does them in accordance with the Sunnah of Allaah's Messenger Muhammad), then he has grasped the most trustworthy handhold [la ilaha ila llaah (none has the right to be worshipped but Allaah)].* ❵-(Surat Luqmaan, from Ayat 22)

And His, The Most High, saying, ❴ *But no, by your Lord, they can have no Faith, until they make you (O Muhammad) judge in all disputes between them, and find in themselves no resistance against your decisions, and accept (them) with full submission.* ❵-(Surat an-Nisaa', Ayat 65)

And the verses in regard to this are many, alhamdulillah. We must remind ourselves that our religion is complete and perfect, alhamdulillah, just as it was revealed to the Last Prophet, Muhammad, may Allaah's praise and salutations be upon him, by the Lord of the Worlds, as He, Glorified and Exalted is He, says,

❴ *This day I have completed your religion for you, and perfected My blessings upon you, and am pleased with Islaam as your religion.* ❵-(Surat al-Maa'idah, Ayat 3)

Sheikh Muhammad ibn 'Abdul Wahab, may Allaah have mercy upon him, has included within his listing of the things which nullify Islaam, *"Abandoning the religion of Allaah, the Most High; not learning about it or acting upon it."* There are two types of abandonment, one which is disbelief, and which causes one to
leave Islaam, and one which does not cause one to immediately leave Islaam, yet is a sin. The lesser abandonment is when one abandons an action that has been legislated, such as the wearing of *hijaab*,

but still believes that it is part of the religion. In this case, the person is committing a sin, but it is not one that takes her outside of Islaam. However, the second type of abandonment, in which one does abandon that which Allaah has legislated through belief that it is not legislated- then this takes one outside of the religion once the proofs have been properly established to you regarding it, may Allaah protect us from that. And falling into the lesser degree of abandonment may lead to the greater abandonment, and to the leaving of Islaam entirely. Both are dangerous, and one must make a reckoning of the state of one's actions and heart on a regular basis, mash'Allaah, in order to rectify our misconceptions and shortcomings as much as we are able, with the help of Allaah.

Along with this, another of those things which nullify Islaam, as mentioned by the Sheikh, is hating something which the Messenger, may Allaah's praise and salutations came with… so how many people hate the *hijaab*, and what is their state in front of Allaah? They must turn to Allaah and ask for His forgiveness, and guidance, and ask Him to replace their hatred with love for an act that has been legislated by the Most Wise, the Most Merciful for the women of this Ummah.

Insh'Allaah, examine these common excuses for abandoning some or all of the *hijaab*, and make a reckoning of your self- your deeds, your speech, and that which is in your heart. Rectify your hearts, and actions, and insh'Allaah your faith will increase, and the benefits be felt in both this life and, most importantly, the next.

The Nakhlah Educational Series: Mission and Methodology (Pocket Edition)

Mission

The Purpose of the 'Nakhlah Educational Series' is to contribute to the present knowledge based efforts which enable Muslim individuals, families, and communities to understand and learn Islaam and then to develop within and truly live Islaam. Our commitment and goal is to contribute beneficial publications and works that:

Firstly, reflect the priority, message and methodology of all the prophets and messengers sent to humanity, meaning that single revealed message which embodies the very purpose of life, and of human creation. As Allaah the Most High has said,

We sent a Messenger to every nation ordering them that they should worship Allaah alone, obey Him and make their worship purely for Him, and that they should avoid everything worshipped besides Allaah. So from them there were those whom Allaah guided to His religion, and there were those who were unbelievers for whom misguidance was ordained. So travel through the land and see the destruction that befell those who denied the Messengers and disbelieved.–(Surah an-Nahl: 36)

Two Essential Foundations

Secondly, building upon the above foundation, our commitment is to contributing publications and works which reflect the inherited message and methodology of the acknowledged scholars of the many various branches of Sharee'ah knowledge who stood upon the straight path of preserved guidance in every century and time since the time of our Messenger, may Allaah's praise and salutations be upon him. These people of knowledge, who are the inheritors of the Final Messenger, have always adhered closely to the two revealed sources of guidance: the Book of Allaah and the Sunnah of the Messenger of Allaah- may Allaah's praise and salutations be upon him, upon the united consensus, standing with the body of guided Muslims in every century - preserving and transmitting the true religion generation after generation. Indeed the Messenger of Allaah, may Allaah's praise and salutations be upon him, informed us that, *{ A group of people amongst my Ummah will remain obedient to Allaah's orders. They will not be harmed by those who leave them nor by those who oppose them, until Allaah's command for the Last Day comes upon them while they remain on the right path. }* (Authentically narrated in Saheeh al-Bukhaaree).

The guiding scholar Sheikh Zayd al-Madkhalee, may Allaah protect him, stated in his writing, 'The Well Established Principles of the Way of the First Generations of Muslims: It's Enduring & Excellent Distinct Characteristics' that,

"From among these principles and characteristics is that the methodology of tasfeeyah -or clarification, and tarbeeyah -or education and cultivation- is clearly affirmed and established as a true way coming from the first three generations of Islaam, and is something well known to the people of true merit from among them, as is concluded by considering all the related evidence. What is intended by tasfeeyah, when referring to it generally, is clarifying that which is the truth from that which is falsehood, what is goodness from that which is harmful and corrupt, and when referring to its specific meanings it is distinguishing the noble Sunnah of the Prophet and the people of the Sunnah from those innovated matters brought into the religion and the people who are supporters of such innovations.

As for what is intended by tarbeeyah, it is calling all of the creation to take on the manners and embrace the excellent character invited to by that guidance revealed to them by their

Lord through His worshiper and Messenger Muhammad, may Allaah's praise and salutations be upon him; so that they might have good character, manners, and behavior. As without this they cannot have a good life, nor can they put right their present condition or their final destination. And we seek refuge in Allaah from the evil of not being able to achieve that rectification."

Thus the methodology of the people of standing upon the Prophet's Sunnah, and proceeding upon the 'way of the believers' in every century is reflected in a focus and concern with these two essential matters: tasfeeyah or clarification of what is original, revealed message from the Lord of all the worlds, and tarbeeyah or education and raising of ourselves, our families, and our communities, and our lands upon what has been distinguished to be that true message and path.

Methodology:

The Roles of the Scholars & General Muslims In Raising the New Generation

The priority and focus of the 'Nakhlah Educational Series' is reflected within in the following statements of Sheikh al-Albaanee, may Allaah have mercy upon him:

"As for the other obligation, then I intend by this the education of the young generation upon Islaam purified from all of those impurities we have mentioned, giving them a correct Islamic education from their very earliest years, without any influence of a foreign, disbelieving education."

(Silsilat al-Hadeeth ad-Da'eefah, Introduction page 2.)

"...And since the Messenger of Allaah, may Allaah's praise and salutations be upon him, has indicated that the only cure to remove this state of humiliation that we find ourselves entrenched within, is truly returning back to the religion. Then it is clearly

obligatory upon us - through the people of knowledge- to correctly and properly understand the religion in a way that conforms to the sources of the Book of Allaah and the Sunnah, and that we educate and raise a new virtuous, righteous generation upon this."

(Clarification and Cultivation and the Need of the Muslims for Them)

It is essential in discussing our perspective upon this obligation of raising the new generation of Muslims, that we highlight and bring attention to a required pillar of these efforts as indicated by Sheikh al-Albaanee, may Allaah have mercy upon him, and others- in the golden words, "*through the people of knowledge*". Since something we commonly experience today is that many people have various incorrect understandings of the role that the scholars should have in the life of a Muslim, failing to understand the way in which they fulfill their position as the inheritors of the Messenger of Allaah, may Allaah's praise and salutations be upon him, and stand as those who preserve and enable us to practice the guidance of Islaam. Similarly the guiding scholar Sheikh 'Abdul-'Azeez Ibn Baaz, may Allaah have mercy upon him, also emphasized this same overall responsibility:

"...It is also upon a Muslim that he struggles diligently in that which will place his worldly affairs in a good state, just as he must also strive in the correcting of his religious affairs and the affairs of his own family. As the people of his household have a significant right over him that he strive diligently in rectifying their affair and guiding them towards goodness, due to the statement of Allaah, the Most Exalted, ❁ **Oh you who believe! Save yourselves and your families Hellfire whose fuel is men and stones** ❁ *-(Surah at-Tahreem: 6)*

So it is upon you to strive to correct the affairs of the members of your family. This includes your wife, your children- both male and female- and such as your own brothers. This concerns all of the people in your family, meaning you should strive to teach them the religion, guiding and directing them, and warning them from those matters Allaah has prohibited for us. Because you are the one who is responsible for them as shown in the statement of the Prophet, may Allaah's praise and salutations be upon him, **{ Every one of you is a guardian, and responsible for what is in his custody. The ruler is a guardian of his subjects and responsible for them; a husband is a guardian of his family and is responsible for it; a lady is a guardian of her husband's house and is responsible for it, and a servant is a guardian of his master's property and is responsible for it....}** *Then the Messenger of Allaah, may Allaah's praise and salutations be upon him, continued to say,* **{...so all of you are guardians and are responsible for those under your authority.}** *(Authentically narrated in Saheeh al-Bukhaaree & Muslim)*

It is upon us to strive diligently in correcting the affairs of the members of our families, from the aspect of purifying their sincerity of intention for Allaah's sake alone in all of their deeds, and ensuring that they truthfully believe in and follow the Messenger of Allaah, may Allaah's praise and salutations be upon him, their fulfilling the prayer and the other obligations which Allaah the Most Exalted has commanded for us, as well as from the direction of distancing them from everything which Allaah has prohibited.

It is upon every single man and women to give advice to their families about the fulfillment of what is obligatory upon them. Certainly, it is upon the woman as well as upon the man to perform this. In this way our homes become corrected and rectified in regard to the most important and essential matters. Allaah said to His Prophet, may Allaah's praise and salutations be upon him, ❰ **And enjoin the ritual prayers on your family...** ❱ *(Surah Taha: 132) Similarly, Allaah the Most Exalted said to*

His prophet Ismaa'aeel, ❦ ***And mention in the Book, Ismaa'aeel. Verily, he was true to what he promised, and he was a Messenger, and a Prophet. And he used to enjoin on his family and his people the ritual prayers and the obligatory charity, and his Lord was pleased with him.*** ❦ *-(Surah Maryam: 54-55)*

As such, it is only proper that we model ourselves after the prophets and the best of people, and be concerned with the state of the members of our households. Do not be neglectful of them, oh worshipper of Allaah! Regardless of whether it is concerning your wife, your mother, father, grandfather, grandmother, your brothers, or your children; it is upon you to strive diligently in correcting their state and condition..."

(Collection of Various Rulings and Statements- Sheikh 'Abdul-'Azeez Ibn 'Abdullah Ibn Baaz, Vol. 6, page 47)

Content & Structure:

We hope to contribute works which enable every striving Muslim who acknowledges the proper position of the scholars, to fulfill the recognized duty and obligation which lays upon each one of us to bring the light of Islaam into our own lives as individuals as well as into our homes and among our families. Towards this goal we are committed to developing educational publications and comprehensive educational curriculums -through cooperation with and based upon the works of the scholars of Islaam and the students of knowledge. Works which, with the assistance of Allaah, the Most High, we can utilize to educate and instruct ourselves, our families and our communities upon Islaam in both principle and practice. The publications and works of the Nakhlah Educational Series are divided into the following categories:

Basic: Ages 4- 6

Elementary: Ages 6-11

Secondary: Ages 11-14

High School: Ages 14- Young Adult

General: Young Adult –Adult

Supplementary: All Ages

Publications and works within these stated levels will, with the permission of Allaah, encompass different beneficial areas and subjects, and will be offered in every permissible form of media and medium. As certainly, as the guiding scholar Sheikh Saaleh Fauzaan al-Fauzaan, may Allaah preserve him, has stated,

"Beneficial knowledge is itself divided into two categories. Firstly is that knowledge which is tremendous in its benefit, as it benefits in this world and continues to benefit in the Hereafter. This is religious Sharee'ah knowledge. And secondly, that which is limited and restricted to matters related to the life of this world, such as learning the processes of manufacturing various goods. This is a category of knowledge related specifically to worldly affairs.

…As for the learning of worldly knowledge, such as knowledge of manufacturing, then it is legislated upon us collectively to learn whatever the Muslims have a need for. Yet If they do not have a need for this knowledge, then learning it is a neutral matter upon the condition that it does not compete with or displace any areas of Sharee'ah knowledge…"

("Explanations of the Mistakes of Some Writers"', Pages 10-12)

We ask Allaah, the most High to bless us with success in contributing to the many efforts of our Muslim brothers and sisters committed to raising themselves as individuals and the next generation of our children upon that Islaam which Allaah has perfected and chosen for us, and which He has enabled the guided Muslims to proceed upon in each and every century. We ask him to forgive us, and forgive the Muslim men and the Muslim women, and to guide all the believers to everything He loves and is pleased with. The success is from Allaah, The Most High The Most Exalted, alone and all praise is due to Him.

Abu Sukhailah Khalil Ibn-Abelahyi
Taalib al-Ilm Educational Resources

BOOK PUBLICATION PREVIEW:

Statements of the Guiding Scholars of Our Age Regarding Books & their Advice to the Beginner Seeker of Knowledge

with Selections from the Following Scholars:
Sheikh 'Abdul-'Azeez ibn 'Abdullah ibn Baaz - Sheikh Muhammad ibn Saaleh al-'Utheimein - Sheikh Muhammad Naasiruddeen al-Albaanee - Sheikh Muqbil ibn Haadee al-Waada'ee - Sheikh 'Abdur-Rahman ibn Naaser as-Sa'adee - Sheikh Muhammad 'Amaan al-Jaamee - Sheikh Muhammad al-Ameen as-Shanqeetee - Sheikh Ahmad ibn Yahya an-Najmee & Sheikh Saaleh al-Fauzaan ibn 'Abdullah al-Fauzaan - Sheikh Saaleh ibn 'Abdul-'Azeez Aal-Sheikh - Sheikh Muhammad ibn 'Abdul-Wahhab al-Wasaabee - Permanent Committee to Scholastic Research & Issuing Of Islamic Rulings

With an introduction by: Sheikh Muhammad Ibn 'Abdullah al-Imaam
Collected and Translated by Abu Sukhailah Khalil Ibn-Abelahyi al-Amreekee

[Available: **Now** ¦ pages: 370+ ¦ price: (S) **$25** (H) **$32** ¦ eBook **$9.99**]

BOOK PUBLICATION PREVIEW:

Al-Waajibaat:
The Obligatory Matters

What it is Decreed that Every Male and Female Muslim Must Have Knowledge Of -from the statements of Sheikh al-Islaam Muhammad ibn 'Abdul-Wahaab

(A Step By Step Course on The Fundamental Beliefs of Islaam- with Lesson Questions, Quizzes, & Exams)

Collected and Arranged by
Umm Mujaahid Khadijah Bint Lacina
al-Amreekiyyah

[Available: **Now** - **Self Study/ Teachers Edition**
price: (Soft cover) **$20** (Hard cover) **$27**
Directed Study Edition price: **$17.50** -
Exercise Workbook price: **$10** ¦ eBook **$9.99**]

BOOK PUBLICATION PREVIEW:

Fasting from Alif to Yaa:
A Day by Day Guide to Making the Most of Ramadhaan

-Contains additional points of benefit to teach one how to live Islaam as a way of life
-Plus, stories of the Prophets and Messengers including activities for the whole family to enjoy and benefit from for each day of Ramadhaan. Some of the Prophets and Messengers covered include Aadam, Ibraaheem, Lut, Yusuf, Sulaymaan, Shu'ayb, Moosa, Zakariyyah, Muhammad, and more! -Recipes for foods enjoyed by Muslims around the world

By Umm Mujaahid Khadijah Bint Lacina al-Amreekiyyah as-Salafiyyah With Abu Hamzah Hudhaifah Ibn Khalil and Umm Usaamah Sukhailah Bint Khalil

|Available: **1433** -pages: 250+ ¦ price: (S) **$20** (H) **$27** ¦
eBook **$9.99**

BOOK PUBLICATION PREVIEW:

My Home, My Path

A Comprehensive Source Book For Today's Muslim Woman Discussing Her Essential Role & Contribution To The Establishment of Islaam – Taken From The Words Of The People Of Knowledge

Collected and Translated by
Umm Mujaahid Khadijah Bint Lacina
al-Amreekiyyah

[Available: **Now** | pages: **420+** | price: (Soft cover) **$22.50** (Hard cover) **$29.50** (eBook) **$9.99**]

BOOK PUBLICATION PREVIEW:

Thalaathatu al-Usool: The Three Fundamental Principles

A Step by Step Educational Course on Islaam Based upon Commentaries of 'Thalaathatu al-Usool' of Sheikh Muhammad ibn 'Abdul Wahaab (may Allaah have mercy upon him)

Collected and Arranged by Umm Mujaahid Khadijah Bint Lacina al-Amreekiyyah

Description:

A complete course for the Believing men and women who want to learn their religion from the ground up, building a firm foundation upon which to base their actions. This is the **second** *in our* **Foundation Series** *on Islamic beliefs and making them a reality in your life, which began with* **"al-Waajibaat: The Obligatory Matters"**.

[Available: **Now Self Study/ Teachers Edition** ¦ price: (Soft cover) **$22.50** (Hard cover) **$29.50** **Directed Study Edition** price: (S) **$17.50** - **Exercise Workbook** price: (S) **$10** ¦ eBook **$9.99**]

PREVIEW

BOOK PUBLICATION PREVIEW:

Whispers of Paradise (1): A Muslim Woman's Life Journal

An Islamic Daily Journal Which Encourages Reflection & Rectification

Collected and Edited by Taalib al-Ilm Educational Resources Development Staff

[Available: **Now** ¦ price: (Hard cover) **$32**]
[Elegantly designed edition is for the year 1434 / 2013]

12 Monthly calendar pages with beneficial quotations from Ibn Qayyim
Daily journal page based upon Islamic calendar (with corresponding C.E. dates)

SCAN WITH SMARTPHONE
FOR MORE INFORMATION

BOOK PUBLICATION PREVIEW:

The Cure, The Explanation, The Clear Affair, & The Brilliantly Distinct Signpost

A Step by Step Educational Course on Islaam Based upon Commentaries of

'Usul as-Sunnah' of Imaam Ahmad

(may Allaah have mercy upon him)

Study of text divided into chapters formatted into multiple short lessons to facilitate learning. Each lesson has: evidence summary, lesson benefits, standard & review exercises 'Usul as-Sunnah' Arabic text & translation divided for easier memorization.

Compiled and Translated by:
Abu Sukhailah Khalil Ibn-Abelahyi

[Available: **TBA** ¦ price: **TBA** (Multi-volume) ¦ soft cover, hard cover, ebook]

www.ingramcontent.com/pod-product-compliance
Lightning Source LLC
Chambersburg PA
CBHW032019040426
42448CB00006B/671